Excel

ADVANCED SKILLS

ENGLISH YEAR 1 AGES 6–7

ADVANCED ENGLISH

Get the Results You Want!

PASCAL PRESS

Donna Gibbs

Contents

Introduction 3
The *Excel* step-by-step improvement plan 4
Excel books to help you *get the results you want!* 5
Question templates and Marking grids 6
Unit 1 8
Unit 2 11
Unit 3 14
Unit 4 17
Unit 5 20
Unit 6 23
Unit 7 26

NAPLAN-style Test 1 29

Unit 8 31
Unit 9 34
Unit 10 37
Unit 11 40
Unit 12 43
Unit 13 46
Unit 14 49
Unit 15 52

NAPLAN-style Test 2 55

Unit 16 57
Unit 17 60
Unit 18 63
Unit 19 66
Unit 20 69
Unit 21 72
Unit 22 75
Unit 23 78

NAPLAN-style Test 3 81

Unit 24 83
Unit 25 86
Unit 26 89
Unit 27 92
Unit 28 95
Unit 29 98
Unit 30 101

NAPLAN-style Test 4 104

Answers 106

Introduction

The aim of the ***Excel* Advanced Skills: Advanced English** series is to build on and extend students' skills in English. Each book in the series supports the requirements of the Australian Curriculum (English) at each year level.

The series consists of six books, one for each year level, from Year 1 to Year 6. The series is supported by other books in the ***Excel* Advanced Skills English** range.

Structure of the book

Each book in the series contains:

- thirty carefully graded, three-page units of teaching and learning activities.
  - **Unit A** includes a sample informative, imaginative or persuasive text and deals with **Reading and comprehension skills**.
  - **Unit B** deals with the Conventions of language: **Spelling**, **Vocabulary**, **Grammar** and **Punctuation**.
  - **Unit C** deals with **Texts in context**. It provides for a deeper analysis and evaluation of the language choices authors make and the ways that readers make meaning from texts.
- four double-page NAPLAN-style tests.
- answers for all questions.

How to use this book

- Students should complete one unit per week. A suggested plan would be to complete the week's Unit A and B page on one day and the Unit C page on another day of the same week.
- After successfully completing a set of units (e.g. 1–7, 8–15, 16–23, 24–30), students should undertake the corresponding NAPLAN-style test.

How to use this book with the *Excel* Advanced Skills: Advanced Mathematics series

For a complete **weekly English and Mathematics program**, use this book in conjunction with the ***Excel* Advanced Skills: Year 1 Advanced Mathematics** book. This way a student will have work set for four days a week: two days for English and two days for Mathematics.

How to assess students' progress

- Templates are included in each book of the series that outline the knowledge and skills targeted by the questions in that book. (Please see page 6.)
- The questions move through the subtopics of English in exactly the same order in each book but as there are more questions and more complex material included in later years of the Year 1 to Year 6 continuum, the question numbers vary across the books.
- The results of the work undertaken in Units A and B can be recorded on the marking grid. See ways to use the marking grid on page 4.

Excel Advanced Skills titles

If students are having difficulty in any area, further support is available in other ***Excel*** workbooks. Please see the comprehensive list on page 5.

The *Excel* step-by-step improvement plan

Step 1

Read the introduction on page 3.

Step 2

Read page 6.

▶ **Question templates**

These outline the knowledge and skills targeted by the questions in the book. Remember that the questions move through the subtopics of English in exactly the same order.

▶ **Marking grids**

The results of the work undertaken in Units A and B can be recorded on the marking grid. This is an easy-to-use diagnostic tool that indicates each student's strengths and weaknesses in relation to specific areas of English.

These results can be used to gather extra information about each student's progress and revision needs. For example, see the sample marking grid for Reading and comprehension in the right-hand column:

- When marking answers on the grid, simply mark incorrect answers with 'X' in the appropriate box. This will result in a graphical representation of areas needing further work. An example for the first five units is shown above. If a question has several parts, it should be counted wrong if one or more mistakes are made.

- Remember that you can identify exactly what type of questions a student is having difficulty with in a topic. For example, in the grid above the student is having difficulty with Reading and comprehension inferring questions.

- There is no marking grid for Unit C.

Marking grid

Reading and comprehension	Literal	Literal	Literal	Inferring	Inferring	Inferring
Question	1	2	3	4	5	6
Unit 1						
Unit 2						X
Unit 3						
Unit 4						X
Unit 5						X
Unit 6						
Unit 7						
Unit 8						
Unit 9						
Unit 10						

This grid indicates that the student needs extra help and practice in inferring questions.

Step 3

Refer to page 5: *Excel* books to help you *get the results you want*!

▶ Under each topic there is a list of books in our range to help students. Each *Excel* book has a comprehensive contents page that will help you find the appropriate pages in the book to target the specific topic you want in each subject area.

Excel books to help you *get the results you want!*

Reading and comprehension

Excel Advanced Skills — READING AND COMPREHENSION WORKBOOK
9781741255683

Excel Basic Skills — Basic Reading Skills
9781741251654

Excel Basic Skills — Reading and Comprehension
9781864413403

Spelling

Excel Advanced Skills — SPELLING AND VOCABULARY WORKBOOK
9781741254648

Excel Handbooks & Guides — Pascal's Basic Primary Spelling
9781864410617

Excel Basic Skills — Spelling, Vocabulary, Grammar and Punctuation
9781864413410

Vocabulary

Excel Advanced Skills — SPELLING AND VOCABULARY WORKBOOK
9781741254648

Excel Basic Skills — Spelling, Vocabulary, Grammar and Punctuation
9781741251654

Grammar

Excel Advanced Skills — GRAMMAR AND PUNCTUATION WORKBOOK
9781741254419

Excel Handbooks & Guides — Pascal's Basic Primary Grammar
9781864410600

Excel Basic Skills — Spelling, Vocabulary, Grammar and Punctuation
9781864413410

Punctuation

Excel Advanced Skills — GRAMMAR AND PUNCTUATION WORKBOOK
9781741254419

Excel Basic Skills — Spelling, Vocabulary, Grammar and Punctuation
9781864413410

Writing

Excel Advanced Skills — WRITING WORKBOOK
9781741254853

Excel Advanced Skills: Year 1 Advanced English

5

Question templates

Reading and comprehension

Q1–3 Literal: Answers to these questions are found directly in the text.

Q4–6 Inferring: Answers to these questions need to be worked out from clues in the text

Spelling

Q1–4 Misspelt words: In these questions, students use their understanding of spelling patterns and spelling rules to correct the mistakes.

Q5 Rhyming words/Word families: In this question, students use their knowledge of word families to build word groups with similar sounds.

Vocabulary

Q6 Synonyms: In this question, students need to recognise similarities of meanings.

Q7 Meanings in context/Word usage: In this question, students need to comprehend the meanings and usage of words in context.

Q8 Definitions: In this question, students are required to demonstrate understanding of word meanings and usage in the context of the text.

Q9 Antonyms: In this question, students need to recognise similarities and differences of word meanings.

Grammar

Q10 Nouns/Noun groups: This question deals with aspects of nouns and noun groups, e.g. common nouns, proper nouns and noun groups with articles.

Q11 Verbs/Verb groups: This question deals with aspects of verbs and verb groups, e.g. person, tense and auxiliary verbs.

Q12 Adverbials: This question deals with adverbials: word groups that tell when, where and how.

Q13 Cohesion: This question deals with words that stand for other words, e.g. pronouns; and words that link ideas across texts, e.g. conjunctions.

Punctuation

Q14–15 These questions deal with ways of punctuating sentences, e.g. adding capital letters, full stops, question marks, exclamation marks, commas, speech marks and apostrophes.

Texts in context

Note: There is no marking grid for Unit C questions.

Q1–6 These questions deal with aspects of text, including:

Purpose and audience: These questions require students to recognise the purpose of a text (such as to inform, persuade or entertain) and the nature of its intended audience (the reader, listener or viewer).

Text structures and features: These questions require students to examine the ways a text is organised through, for example, sequencing, paragraphing and cohesive devices.

Textual interpretations: These questions require students to analyse the text and its effectiveness through, for example, language choices, imagery and point of view.

Get creative

Q7 This task requires students to create their own texts by adding to or responding to the models provided. Student responses will vary as this task is open-ended.

This icon indicates where students will need to use their own paper to answer the question.

Marking grid

Reading and comprehension						
	Literal	Literal	Literal	Inferring	Inferring	Inferring
Question	1	2	3	4	5	6
Unit 1						
Unit 2						
Unit 3						
Unit 4						
Unit 5						
Unit 6						
Unit 7						
Unit 8						
Unit 9						
Unit 10						
Unit 11						
Unit 12						
Unit 13						
Unit 14						
Unit 15						
Unit 16						
Unit 17						
Unit 18						
Unit 19						
Unit 20						
Unit 21						
Unit 22						
Unit 23						
Unit 24						
Unit 25						
Unit 26						
Unit 27						
Unit 28						
Unit 29						
Unit 30						
Question	1	2	3	4	5	6

Marking grid

Conventions of language	Spelling					Vocabulary				Grammar				Punctuation	
	Misspelt words	Misspelt words	Misspelt words	Misspelt words	Rhyming words / Word families	Synonyms	Meanings in context / Word usage	Definitions	Antonyms	Nouns / Noun groups	Verbs / Verb groups	Adverbials	Cohesion	Punctuation	Punctuation
Question	1	2	3	4	5	6	7	8	9	10	11	12	13	14	15
Unit 1															
Unit 2															
Unit 3															
Unit 4															
Unit 5															
Unit 6															
Unit 7															
Unit 8															
Unit 9															
Unit 10															
Unit 11															
Unit 12															
Unit 13															
Unit 14															
Unit 15															
Unit 16															
Unit 17															
Unit 18															
Unit 19															
Unit 20															
Unit 21															
Unit 22															
Unit 23															
Unit 24															
Unit 25															
Unit 26															
Unit 27															
Unit 28															
Unit 29															
Unit 30															
Question	1	2	3	4	5	6	7	8	9	10	11	12	13	14	15

Excel **Advanced Skills: Year 1 Advanced English**

READING AND COMPREHENSION

UNIT 1A

Tom's lost cat

1
2 My cat, Sally, is lost. Where can she be?
3 I look under the table. I look under my bed.
4 Not there. I look at the rug near the fire.
5 I look on top of the television. Not there.
6 Then I look outside and see the dog from
7 next door. He's barking loudly at a tall tree
8 in our yard. I think I've found my cat!

1. What is lost?
   - **A** a cat
   - **B** a dog
   - **C** a rug

2. What does Tom look on top of?
   - **A** the table
   - **B** the bed
   - **C** the television

3. What is the first thing Tom sees when he looks outside?
   - **A** his cat
   - **B** a dog
   - **C** a tree

4. Why does Tom look outside?
   - **A** He hears his cat.
   - **B** He can't find his cat inside.
   - **C** He sees the dog.

5. Why does the dog bark loudly?
   - **A** He sees the cat up the tree.
   - **B** He is hungry.
   - **C** He is scared by Tom.

6. Where does Tom think his cat is?

....

....

....

....

Answers and explanations on page 106

Excel Advanced Skills: Year 1 Advanced English

UNIT 1B

SPELLING

Unscramble the letters to make words from the text in questions 1–4.

1 gur

2 frie

3 kool

4 eetr

5 Write three words that end with **ot**.

VOCABULARY

6 Circle the word that has a similar meaning to the underlined word.

I look under the table.
- A over
- B down
- C beneath
- D outside

7 Add a word from the text to the sentence.

_____ is my cat?

8 Which word from the text means **can't be found**?

9 Circle the word that does **not** belong.
- A big
- B tall
- C short
- D long

GRAMMAR

10 Add labels to the picture with common nouns from the text.

11 Choose a verb from the box to correctly complete the sentence.

| saw | see | sees | seeing |

Did you _____ my cat?

12 Write words from the text to tell **where**.

There is a tall tree _____.

13 Choose a pronoun from the box to correctly complete the sentence.

| he | she | it | you | they | I | we |

Tom looks inside and then _____ looks outside.

PUNCTUATION

Rewrite the sentences correctly.

14 i think my cat is lost

15 you can see the dog from next door

Answers and explanations on page 106

Excel Advanced Skills: Year 1 Advanced English

TEXTS IN CONTEXT

UNIT 1C

Tom's lost cat

1
2 My cat, Sally, is lost. Where can she be?
3 I look under the table. I look under my bed.
4 Not there. I look at the rug near the fire.
5 I look on top of the television. Not there.
6 Then I look outside and see the dog from
7 next door. He's barking loudly at a tall tree
8 in our yard. I think I've found my cat!

---

1. This text is about
   A why dogs chase cats.
   B looking for a lost cat.
   C how to look after a cat.

2. In this text Tom
   A describes his cat.
   B tells how to lose a cat.
   C recounts what he did.

3. In what order do these things happen?
   A Tom sees the dog.
   B Tom loses his cat.
   C Tom thinks he has found his cat.

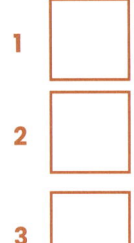

   1 ☐
   2 ☐
   3 ☐

4. The words 'look' and 'not there' are repeated to show
   A what fun Tom is having.
   B how sad Tom is feeling.
   C how hard Tom is trying.

5. The exclamation in the text (line 8) is used to express Tom's
   A anger.
   B surprise.
   C sadness.

6. Tom's actions show he is a _____ pet owner.
   A careful
   B careless
   C carefree

Get creative

7. Draw a picture of Tom looking for his cat. Write a caption for your drawing.

Answers and explanations on page 106

10

Excel Advanced Skills: Year 1 Advanced English

READING AND COMPREHENSION

UNIT 2A

My little brother

My little brother, James, has just started at preschool. I don't go to preschool anymore. I'm in Year One and my new teacher is called Mr Thomas. I like him.

Our school is next door to the preschool. Sometimes I go to the fence and hold on to it with my fingers. Then I can lift my head to see if James is in the playground with his friends. If he sees me, he calls out "Hello Libby". Luckily he is too little to climb over the fence!

1. James is Libby's
   A big brother.
   B little brother.
   C twin brother.

2. Libby is in
   A preschool.
   B Kindergarten.
   C Year One.

3. The school is _____ the preschool.
   A across the road from
   B next door to
   C a long way from

4. How does Libby feel about being in Year One?
   A happy
   B unhappy
   C sad

5. How does James feel about Libby?
   A He dislikes her.
   B He thinks she is a show-off.
   C He is fond of her.

6. Why is it lucky that James can't climb the fence?

UNIT 2B

SPELLING

Unscramble the letters to make words from the text in questions 1–4.

1. ym

2. meco

3. bmicl

4. ttleli

5. Write three words that end with **an**.

VOCABULARY

6. Circle the word that has a similar meaning to the underlined word.

   I can see you if I lift my head up high.
   - A carry
   - B raise
   - C bend
   - D push

7. Add a word from the text to the sentence.

   My new teacher is ____ Mr Thomas.

8. Which word from the text means **now and then**?

9. Circle the word that does **not** belong.
   - A hold
   - B grip
   - C drop
   - D grasp

GRAMMAR

10. Add labels to the picture with common nouns from the text.

11. Choose a verb from the box to correctly complete the sentence.

    | starts | starting | started | start |

    My brother ____ at preschool last week.

12. Write words from the text to tell **where**.

    Is James playing ____ today?

13. Choose a pronoun from the box to correctly complete the sentence.

    | he | she | it | you | they | I | we |

    I held on with my fingers because ____ are very strong.

PUNCTUATION

Rewrite the sentences correctly.

14. i like my new teacher

15. james likes preschool

Answers and explanations on page 106

UNIT 2C

TEXTS IN CONTEXT

1 **My little brother**

2 My little brother, James, has just started at preschool. I don't go to
3 preschool anymore. I'm in Year One and my new teacher is called
4 Mr Thomas. I like him.

5 Our school is next door to the preschool. Sometimes I go to the fence
6 and hold on to it with my fingers. Then I can lift my head to see if
7 James is in the playground with his friends. If he sees me, he calls out
8 "Hello Libby". Luckily he is too little to climb over the fence!

1 The text is about
   A Mum and Dad.
   B James and Libby.
   C Mr and Mrs Thomas.

2 Who wrote this text?
   A Libby
   B James
   C Mr Thomas

3 Whose eyes can you see in the picture?
   A James's
   B Libby's
   C Mum's

4 The exclamation (line 8) is used to show
   A strong feeling.
   B shock.
   C surprise.

5 Mum and Dad would like this text because it shows their children
   A break the rules.
   B dislike each other.
   C are happy at their schools.

6 The last sentence (line 8) makes the reader
   A cry.
   B smile.
   C worry.

Get creative

7 Draw a picture of what Libby sees when she looks over the fence.

Answers and explanations on pages 106–107

Excel Advanced Skills: Year 1 Advanced English

READING AND COMPREHENSION

UNIT 3A

1 **My best friend**

2 Flo is my best friend. She has black hair and eyes that twinkle. She is
3 a tiny bit taller than I am. Flo rides her bike to my house. We like to
4 play skipping and hopscotch. We also sit on the fence and look at the
5 clouds. Once Flo said she saw a dragon in the sky. I wish I'd seen a
6 dragon. Flo is kind to me. I hope we stay friends always.

7 by Violet

1 What colour is Flo's hair?
   A fair   B brown   C black

2 What did Flo say she saw?
   A a friend   B a dragon   C the sky

3 What do Flo and Violet sit on?
   A the fence   B the clouds   C Flo's bike

4 Why does Violet like Flo?
   A They have the same colour hair.
   B She plays hopscotch.
   C They like doing the same things.

5 Flo and Violet like spending time
   A outdoors.   B at school.   C indoors.

6 Why does Violet hope she will always be friends with Flo?

....

....

Answers and explanations on page 107

14

Excel Advanced Skills: **Year 1 Advanced English**

UNIT 3B

SPELLING

Unscramble the letters to make words from the text in questions 1–4.

1 steb

2 yees

3 kbie

4 drgaon

5 Write three words that end with **it**.

VOCABULARY

6 Circle the word that has a similar meaning to the underlined word.

   I hope I will be Flo's friend <u>always</u>.
   - A never
   - B sometimes
   - C forever
   - D often

7 Add a word from the text to the sentence.

   We like to look at the .... in the sky.

8 Which word from the text means **one time only**?

9 Circle the word that does **not** belong.
   - A twinkle
   - B sparkle
   - C shine
   - D burn

GRAMMAR

10 Add labels to the picture with common nouns from the text.

11 Choose a verb from the box to correctly complete the sentence.

| playing | played | play | plays |

   Violet and Flo like to .... games together.

12 Write words from the text to tell **where**.

   Flo saw a dragon ....

13 Choose a pronoun from the box to correctly complete the sentence.

| he | she | it | you | they | I | we |

   Flo and Violet sit on the fence and .... watch the clouds.

PUNCTUATION

Rewrite the sentences correctly.

14 flo is my best friend

15 violet is not as tall as flo

👉 Answers and explanations on page 107

Excel Advanced Skills: Year 1 Advanced English

UNIT 3C

TEXTS IN CONTEXT

1 **My best friend**

2 Flo is my best friend. She has black hair and eyes that twinkle. She is
3 a tiny bit taller than I am. Flo rides her bike to my house. We like to
4 play skipping and hopscotch. We also sit on the fence and look at the
5 clouds. Once Flo said she saw a dragon in the sky. I wish I'd seen a
6 dragon. Flo is kind to me. I hope we stay friends always.

7 by Violet

1. This text is about
   A how to be a good friend.
   B games to play with a friend.
   C what Violet thinks of Flo as a friend.

2. This text would be found in a
   A photo album.
   B diary.
   C book of fairytales.

3. The part that describes what Flo looks like is
   A early in the text.
   B in the middle of the text.
   C at the end of the text.

4. The text mainly
   A expresses thoughts and feelings.
   B gives arguments for and against.
   C gives a list of events.

5. Which words from the text best describe Flo's nature?
   A She is kind to me.
   B She rides her bike.
   C She is Violet's best friend.

6. The picture
   A adds lots of new information.
   B is not closely linked to the text.
   C mainly shows what is in the text.

Get creative

7. Draw a picture of a friend. Then write a sentence about why you like your friend.

Answers and explanations on page 107

16

Excel Advanced Skills: Year 1 Advanced English

READING AND COMPREHENSION

UNIT 4A

1 **Emus**

2 Emus are big, tall birds. They
3 cannot fly. Their necks and legs
4 are long but their wings are small.
5 They have brown feathers. They
6 like to eat plants and insects. The
7 mother emus lay between six and
8 11 eggs in the grass. These take
9 about 60 days to hatch. The father
10 emus sit on the eggs. The fathers
11 also look after the baby emus until
12 they are about two years old.

1 Emus are
   A short.
   B wide.
   C tall.

2 What do emus eat?
   A eggs
   B plants
   C feathers

3 How long do emu eggs take to hatch?
   A between six and 11 days
   B about 60 days
   C about two years

4 Why is it too hard for emus to fly?
   A Their wings are small.
   B They dislike flying.
   C They aren't very strong.

5 What would help emus run fast?
   A their brown feathers
   B their small heads
   C their long legs

6 Why does a parent sit on the eggs?
   A to have a rest
   B to keep the eggs warm
   C to keep cool in the grass

Answers and explanations on page 107

Excel Advanced Skills: Year 1 Advanced English

UNIT 4B

SPELLING

Unscramble the letters to make words from the text in questions 1–4.

1. klie

   ....

2. llsma

   ....

3. muse

   ....

4. yads

   ....

5. Write three words that end with **ay**.

   ....

   ....

VOCABULARY

6. Circle the word that has a similar meaning to the underlined word.

   The father sits on the eggs and cares for the baby chicks <u>also</u>.

   A too   B more
   C again   D well

7. Add a word from the text to the sentence.

   The father emu looks after the

   .... emus.

8. Which word from the text means **small animals whose bodies have three parts and six legs?**

   ....

9. Circle the word that does **not** belong.

   A hate
   B dislike
   C like
   D detest

GRAMMAR

10. Add labels to the picture with common nouns from the text.

11. Choose a verb from the box to correctly complete the sentence.

    | have | had | has | having |

    Emus .... strong legs.

12. Write words from the text to tell **where**.

    The mother lays her eggs ....

    ....

13. Choose a pronoun from the box to correctly complete the sentence.

    | he | she | it | you | they | I | we |

    The father emu sits on the eggs and

    .... helps look after the chicks.

PUNCTUATION

Rewrite the sentences correctly.

14. baby emus hatch from eggs

    ....

    ....

15. the emu is a very tall bird

    ....

    ....

Answers and explanations on page 107

Excel Advanced Skills: Year 1 Advanced English

TEXTS IN CONTEXT

UNIT 4C

1 **Emus**

2 Emus are big, tall birds. They
3 cannot fly. Their necks and legs
4 are long but their wings are small.
5 They have brown feathers. They
6 like to eat plants and insects. The
7 mother emus lay between 6 and 11
8 eggs in the grass. These take about
9 60 days to hatch. The father emus
10 sit on the eggs. The fathers also
11 look after the baby emus until they
12 are about two years old.

1. This text mainly
   A tells a story.
   B gives information.
   C is a discussion.

2. Where would you find this text?
   A in a comic
   B on the television
   C in a book about birds

3. The numbers in the text tell about
   A amounts.
   B length of time.
   C amounts and length of time.

4. The describing words in the text mainly tell
   A what emus look like.
   B how emus behave.
   C where emus live.

5. The word **about** is used three times because what it tells
   A can't be measured exactly.
   B can be measured exactly.
   C is information no-one has.

6. The picture is a useful addition to the text because it shows
   A that emus have shadows.
   B where emus live.
   C how quickly emus can move.

Get creative

7. Find out another fact about emus. Write a new sentence about this information. Draw a picture to illustrate your new information.

Answers and explanations on pages 107–108

19

Excel Advanced Skills: Year 1 Advanced English

READING AND COMPREHENSION

UNIT 5A

1 **Road safety**

2 A policewoman came to our class
3 today. She talked to us about safety
4 on the roads.

5 She asked, "What does the colour
6 red mean, George?"

7 "It means stop. Don't cross the road," I said.

8 "And what colour must you wait for to cross the road, Tim?"

9 "Green," said my friend.

10 "What MUST you wear when you ride your bikes?"

11 "Our helmets," the class called out.

12 "Very good. Always stay safe," the policewoman said to us with a
13 friendly smile.

1. Which colour means stop?
   - A red
   - B yellow
   - C green

2. What must you wear when you ride a bike?
   - A a red jumper
   - B a helmet
   - C a smile

3. What kind of safety did the policewoman talk about?
   - A safety in the bush
   - B safety in the water
   - C safety on the roads

4. The policewoman spoke in a _____ way to the children.
   - A strict
   - B friendly
   - C cross

5. The policewoman asked the children questions because
   - A she didn't know the answers.
   - B she wanted to be sure they knew the answers.
   - C she wanted to trick them.

6. What would help the children 'Always stay safe' (line 12)?

Answers and explanations on page 108

Excel Advanced Skills: Year 1 Advanced English

UNIT 5B

SPELLING

Unscramble the letters to make words from the text in questions 1–4.

1. tmus

2. ssroc

3. lassc

4. eenrg

5. Write three words that end with **ed**.

VOCABULARY

6. Circle the word that has a similar meaning to the underlined word.

   I liked her <u>friendly</u> smile.
   - A warm
   - B cool
   - C cold
   - D unkind

7. Add a word from the text to the sentence.

   We learned about _____ on the roads.

8. Which word from the text means **a group of students with a teacher**?

9. Circle the word that does **not** belong.
   - A stop
   - B pause
   - C go
   - D stay

GRAMMAR

10. Add labels to the picture with common nouns from the text.

11. Choose a verb from the box to correctly complete the sentence.

    | comes | coming | came | come |

    A policewoman _____ to talk to us at school earlier today.

12. Write words from the text to tell **where**.

    We must remember to stay safe _____.

13. Choose a pronoun from the box to correctly complete the sentence.

    | he | she | it | you | they | I | we |

    The policewoman was friendly and _____ told us how to be safe.

PUNCTUATION

Rewrite the sentences correctly.

14. it is important to know the rules

15. does she have a new bike helmet

Answers and explanations on page 108

21

Excel Advanced Skills: Year 1 Advanced English

UNIT 5C

> TEXTS IN CONTEXT

1 **Road safety**

2 A policewoman came to our class
3 today. She talked to us about safety
4 on the roads.

5 She asked, "What does the colour
6 red mean, George?"

7 "It means stop. Don't cross the road," I said.

8 "And what colour must you wait for to cross the road, Tim?"

9 "Green," said my friend.

10 "What MUST you wear when you ride your bikes?"

11 "Our helmets," the class called out.

12 "Very good. Always stay safe," the policewoman said to us with a
13 friendly smile.

---

1. This text is about
   A what to wear to be safe on the road.
   B how to learn the rules of the road.
   C the rules of the road.

2. Who tells the reader about the visit?
   A George   B Tim   C the class

3. In which order did these events happen?
   A The class answered a question.
   B Tim answered a question.
   C George answered a question.

   1 ☐   2 ☐   3 ☐

4. The word 'MUST' (line 10) is in capital letters to show
   A how important it is.
   B it is a proper noun.
   C the policewoman is shouting.

5. Why does the class call out the answer (line 11)?
   A to show they know everything
   B to show they know the answer very well
   C to show off

6. How do you know the policewoman has visited the class before?

   ....
   ....
   ....

Get creative

7. Write down another thing that it is important to do to keep safe on the roads. Ask an adult for help if you are unsure.

☞ Answers and explanations on page 108

READING AND COMPREHENSION

UNIT 6A

Rock art

❶ Rock art is made up of paintings or carvings on rock. It is found all over the world. You can see Aboriginal rock art in many parts of Australia. This rock art tells stories about the lives of their people. The pictures are often of animals such as kangaroos, turtles and emus.

❷ The handprints in the picture below were found on rocks in northern Australia. They are thousands of years old.

❸ One way these handprints were made was by painting the hand and fingers with a clay-like mixture. Then the hand was pressed into the rock. When it was lifted up, its print was left behind.

1. Rock art is found
   - A only in Australia.
   - B all over the world.
   - C in one or two countries.

2. The picture above was painted
   - A today.
   - B yesterday.
   - C thousands of years ago.

3. Rock art is
   - A a group of rocks.
   - B paintings or carvings on rocks.
   - C paintings of animals.

4. How many fingers are in the rock painting of hands?
   - A five
   - B ten
   - C fifteen

5. The small hand in the picture is likely to belong to
   - A a child.
   - B a woman.
   - C a man.

6. Why were pictures of animals common in Aboriginal rock art?

....
....

☞ Answers and explanations on page 108

UNIT 6B

SPELLING

Unscramble the letters to make words from the text in questions 1–4.

1. ckro

   ....

2. andsh

   ....

3. ingfers

   ....

4. Atrusalia

   ....

5. Write three words that end with **in**.

   ....

   ....

VOCABULARY

6. Circle the word that has a similar meaning to the underlined word.

   The paintings were <u>found</u> in northern Australia.

   A discovered   B seen
   C watched   D left

7. Add a word from the text to the sentence.

   They painted their hands then .... them into the rock.

8. Which word from the text means **something made by mixing things together**?

   ....

9. Circle the word or word group that does **not** belong.

   A above
   B below
   C on top of
   D higher up than

GRAMMAR

10. Add labels to the picture with common nouns from the text.

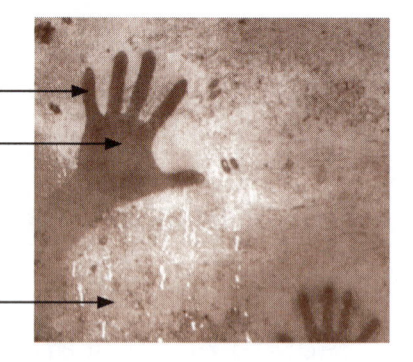

11. Choose a verb from the box to correctly complete the sentence.

    | were | are | is | was |

    The picture .... painted a long time ago.

12. Write words from the text to tell **where**.

    Rock art is found ....

    ....

13. Choose a pronoun from the box to correctly complete the sentence.

    | he | she | it | you | they | I | we |

    He pressed his hand into the rock then lifted .... off.

PUNCTUATION

Rewrite the sentences correctly.

14. did you see the rock art

    ....

    ....

15. they painted pictures of animals

    ....

    ....

Answers and explanations on page 108

TEXTS IN CONTEXT

UNIT 6C

Rock art

❶ Rock art is made up of paintings or carvings on rock. It is found all over the world. You can see Indigenous rock art in many parts of Australia. This rock art tells stories about the lives of their people. The pictures are often of animals such as kangaroos, turtles and emus.

❷ The handprints in the picture below were found on rocks in northern Australia. They are thousands of years old.

❸ One way these handprints were made was by painting the hand and fingers with a clay-like mixture. Then the hand was pressed into the rock. When it was lifted up, its print was left behind.

1. This text was written to
   A sell rock art.
   B give factual information about rock art.
   C tell stories about rock art.

2. You would be likely to find this text in
   A a book about art.
   B junk mail.
   C a newspaper.

3. The text begins by
   A describing Indigenous rock art.
   B explaining what rock art is.
   C telling when people made rock art.

4. To which paragraph could you add another way of making handprints?
   A paragraph one
   B paragraph two
   C paragraph three

5. Indigenous rock art is _____ rock art from around the world.
   A the only
   B an example of
   C the same as

6. Do you think rock art is interesting? Why or why not?

Get creative

7. Get a large piece of blank paper. Draw around the shape of your hand. Draw around the hands of friends or other people in your family. Paint the background and put your picture on display.

Answers and explanations on pages 108–109

25

Excel Advanced Skills: Year 1 Advanced English

UNIT 7A

READING AND COMPREHENSION

Banana pancakes

Remember to have an adult nearby when using the stove.

You need:
1½ cups milk
1 egg
2 cups self-raising flour
2 mashed bananas
25 grams butter
Nuts and honey

Method:
- Whisk milk and egg together in a jug.
- Sift flour into a bowl. Add milk mixture and mix together. Add bananas.
- Heat a non-stick frying pan over medium heat and brush pan with butter.
- Pour ¼ cup mixture into the pan to cook. Turn over when browned. Remove to a plate when both sides are cooked and put in oven to keep warm. Repeat until all the mixture is used.
- Add nuts and honey. Serve.

1. How much milk do you need?
   A 1 cup
   B 1½ cups
   C 2 cups

2. What kind of frying pan is used?
   A huge
   B cool
   C non-stick

3. You have to _____ the bananas.
   A mash
   B slice
   C chop

4. Why is an adult needed nearby?
   A to help whisk and mash
   B because using a stove can be dangerous
   C to help pour the mixture

5. The mixture is likely to be
   A a bit runny.
   B stiff and hard.
   C like cement.

6. Do you think you could make pancakes? Why or why not? _____

Answers and explanations on page 109

Excel Advanced Skills: Year 1 Advanced English

UNIT 7B

SPELLING

Unscramble the letters to make words from the text in questions 1–4.

1. etovs

2. nanabas

3. peatre

4. nohye

5. Write three words that end with **ug**.

VOCABULARY

6. Circle the word that has a similar meaning to the underlined word.

   You have to use a medium heat.
   - A warm
   - B middling
   - C very hot
   - D fiery

7. Add a word from the text to the sentence.

   You can .... the pancakes with nuts and honey.

8. Which word from the text means **grown up**?

9. Circle the word that does **not** belong.
   - A remember
   - B recall
   - C remind
   - D forget

GRAMMAR

10. Add labels to the picture with common nouns from the text.

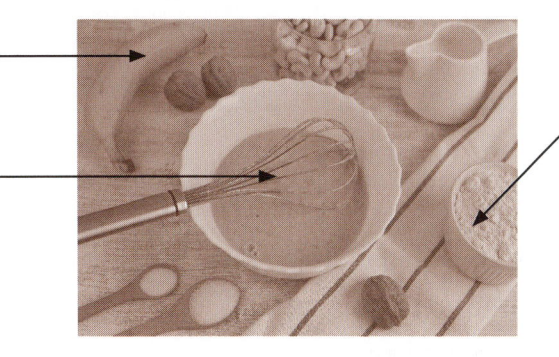

11. Choose a verb from the box to correctly complete the sentence.

    | needs | need | needing | needed |

    You also .... to have a jug, a bowl and a frying pan ready.

12. Write words from the text to tell **where**.

    Pour some mixture ....

13. Choose a pronoun from the box to correctly complete the sentence.

    | he | she | it | you | they | I | we |

    It's good to add bananas because .... make the pancakes moist.

PUNCTUATION

Rewrite the sentences correctly.

14. we had banana pancakes for breakfast

15. he did not want nuts or honey

Answers and explanations on page 109

27

Excel Advanced Skills: Year 1 Advanced English

UNIT 7C

TEXTS IN CONTEXT

1 **Banana pancakes**
2 Remember to have an adult nearby when using the stove.
3 **You need:**
4 1½ cups milk
5 1 egg
6 2 cups self-raising flour
7 2 mashed bananas
8 25 grams butter
9 Nuts and honey
10 **Method:**
11 • Whisk milk and egg together in a jug.
12 • Sift flour into a bowl. Add milk mixture and mix together. Add bananas.
13 • Heat a non-stick frying pan over medium heat and brush pan with butter.
14 • Pour ¼ cup mixture into the pan to cook. Turn over when browned.
15   Remove to a plate when both sides are cooked and put in oven to keep
16   warm. Repeat until all the mixture is used.
17 • Add nuts and honey. Serve.

1 This text tells you
   A why you should make pancakes.
   B when to make pancakes.
   C how to make pancakes.

2 You would find this text in
   A an adult cookbook.
   B a children's cookbook.
   C a calendar.

3 The foods you need are listed
   A in order of their weight.
   B in the order you use them.
   C in order of their size.

4 Which is a rule that must always be followed?
   A Remember to have an adult nearby when using the stove. (line 2)
   B Repeat until all the mixture is used. (line 16)
   C Add nuts and honey. (line 17)

5 What is **not** listed?
   A the steps to follow
   B the food (e.g. eggs, flour) you need
   C the utensils (e.g. whisk, pan) you need

6 Does the picture suit the text? Why or why not?

   ....
   ....
   ....

Get creative

7 Borrow a book of recipes for children from the library or search for recipes on the internet. Choose a recipe you would like to try. Write its name here:

   ....

☞ Answers and explanations on page 109

Excel Advanced Skills: Year 1 Advanced English

NAPLAN-style Reading Test 1

When I grow up

Today Mum showed us how to make buns. Ben and I wore our aprons and our hats. I learned how to crack the eggs into the bowl. Ben kept trying to taste the mixture before it was cooked!

When I grow up I'm going to be a cook. Already I can boil an egg, make toast and cook pancakes. My brother says he wants to be a cook too. I think he is just copying me. I don't think he'd be a very good cook because he spills things. I'm going to have my own café. I hope I will get lots of customers.

by Sylvia

1. What are the children learning to cook?
   A pancakes
   B eggs
   C buns

2. When did they have their cooking lesson?
   A today
   B tomorrow
   C yesterday

3. Why does Sylvia think Ben would not be a good cook?
   A He is her brother.
   B He spills things.
   C He is younger than she is.

4. Did Mum, Sylvia and Ben all wear aprons and hats?
   A yes
   B no
   C maybe

5. Who is the 'I' in the title?
   A Sylvia
   B Mum
   C Ben

6. Which statement is true?
   A Ben doesn't want to be a cook.
   B Mum thinks Ben will be a better cook than Sylvia.
   C Sylvia thinks she will be a better cook than Ben.

7. Where would you read this text?
   A in a magazine
   B in a cookbook
   C in a diary

Answers and explanations on page 109

NAPLAN-style Conventions of Language Test 1

Each sentence has one word that is incorrect. Write the correct spelling of each word.

1. Is that yore dog by the fence?

   ....

2. I live in a howse next to the shops.

   ....

3. My freind is taller than I am.

   ....

4. Mum sais we can play football in the park.

   ....

5. I don't think you shood do that!

   ....

Read the text. Choose the correct word to complete the sentences.

Yoga for children

Elly came to play at my house ......(6)....... . I live on a farm. Elly and I love running in the fields. ......(7)....... like playing with the dogs. They chase after us and make us run ......(8)....... .

6. A tomorrow   B then
   C soon   D yesterday

7. A We   B She
   C They   D Them

8. A quick   B quickly
   C quicker   D quickest

9. Which word is a common noun?

   I always like playing at the playground near us.
   A always   B like
   C playing   D playground

10. Choose the correct verb or verb group to complete the sentence.

    Dinosaurs .... a long, long time ago.
    A are living   B live
    C lived   D was living

11. Underline the words that tell **where**.

    She boiled the kettle then poured the water into the cup.

12. Which pronoun correctly completes the sentence?

    Bill gave Millie an apple and .... said thank you.
    A he   B she
    C they   D we

13. Which sentence is punctuated correctly?
    A Did you see the baby kitten?
    B Did you see the baby kitten.
    C Did you see the baby kitten!
    D Did you see the Baby Kitten?

14. Which sentence is punctuated correctly?
    A Sadie and angus are at the swimming pool.
    B Sadie and Angus are at the Swimming Pool.
    C Sadie and Angus are at the swimming Pool.
    D Sadie and Angus are at the swimming pool.

Answers and explanations on page 109

READING AND COMPREHENSION

UNIT 8A

1 **Come to our garage sale**
2 **When:** Saturday 18 June, 9 am—until everything is sold
3 **Where:** 12 Merry St, Chipville, South Australia
4 **What:** Toys, books, clothes, kitchen utensils, rugs, furniture, camping gear,
5 sporting gear, fishing gear, diving gear, tools and MORE. Chocolate brownies
6 made by my gran will be on sale and there will also be a lucky dip.
7 **Why:** My name is Jimmy and I hope you will come to our garage sale. We
8 are moving to Malaysia to live for a few years and we can't take all this
9 stuff with us.
10 PS: Please don't buy my train set because I really want to keep it!

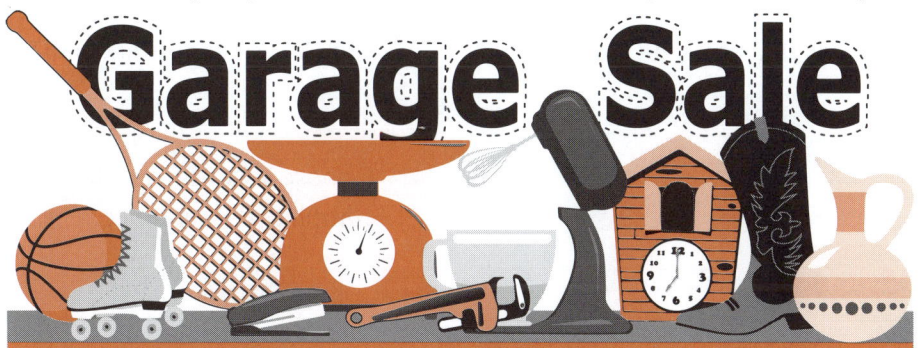

1 Where is the family moving?
   A Merry St   B Chipville   C Malaysia

2 Who wrote this text?
   A Jimmy's parents   B Jimmy   C Jimmy's gran

3 Jimmy thinks the sale will finish
   A when everything is sold.   B at the end of the morning.   C at the end of the weekend.

4 Jimmy is _____ that someone will buy his train set.
   A hopeful   B worried   C certain

5 The picture aims to attract
   A adults.
   B children.
   C adults and children.

6 Would you like to go to this garage sale? Why or why not?

Answers and explanations on pages 109–110

Excel Advanced Skills: Year 1 Advanced English

UNIT 8B

SPELLING

Write the correct spelling of the underlined words in questions 1–4.

1. I'd like the scales for my <u>kichen</u>.

   ....

2. Did they have any sporting <u>geer</u> for sale?

   ....

3. His gran cooked <u>chocklate</u> brownies.

   ....

4. Jimmy wrote the notice for their garage <u>sail</u>.

   ....

5. Write three words that end with **un**.

   ....

   ....

VOCABULARY

6. Circle the word that has a similar meaning to the underlined word.

   Our family has diving <u>gear</u> for sale.
   - A bags
   - B luggage
   - C outfits
   - D parcels

7. Which word from the text means **not many but more than one**?

   ....

8. Add a word from the text to the sentence.

   We usually keep our car in the ....

9. Circle the word that does **not** belong.
   - A fear
   - B worry
   - C dread
   - D hope

GRAMMAR

10. Complete the sentence with a common noun from the text.

    We are moving to Malaysia for a few ....

11. Choose a verb from the box to correctly complete the sentence.

    | took | taken | take | takes |

    We can't .... everything with us.

12. Write words from the text to tell **when**.

    The date of our garage sale is ....

13. Choose a word from the box to correctly complete the sentence.

    | and | so | but | because | or |

    I hope you won't buy my train set .... I want to keep it.

PUNCTUATION

Rewrite the sentences correctly.

14. will you buy any toys

    ....

    ....

15. have you ever had a garage sale

    ....

    ....

Answers and explanations on page 110

UNIT 8C

TEXTS IN CONTEXT

1. **Come to our garage sale**
2. **When:** Saturday 18 June, 9 am—until everything is sold
3. **Where:** 12 Merry St, Chipville, South Australia
4. **What:** Toys, books, clothes, kitchen utensils, rugs, furniture, camping gear,
5. sporting gear, fishing gear, diving gear, tools and MORE. Chocolate brownies
6. made by my gran will be on sale and there will also be a lucky dip.
7. **Why:** My name is Jimmy and I hope you will come to our garage sale. We
8. are moving to Malaysia to live for a few years and we can't take all this
9. stuff with us.
10. **PS:** Please don't buy my train set because I really want to keep it!

1. The purpose of the text is to
   A persuade the reader to do something.
   B share thoughts and feelings with the reader.
   C tell the reader how to do something.

2. The text is
   A a review.
   B an advertisement.
   C a diary entry.

3. The text is mainly organised
   A under headings.
   B in time order.
   C as a list of events.

4. The word 'MORE' (line 5) is in capital letters
   A to explain that you can buy more things.
   B to suggest there'll be a huge number of things to choose from.
   C to hide the fact that Jimmy forgets what else there is to sell.

5. Which section has the most personal information included in it?
   A the **Where** section
   B the **What** section
   C the **Why** section

6. If Jimmy's parents decided to edit his notice, which sentence would they be likely to remove?

   _____
   _____

Get creative

7. Pretend your family is going to have a garage sale. Make a 'For Sale' notice to put on the noticeboard at your local shopping centre.

Answers and explanations on page 110

Excel Advanced Skills: Year 1 Advanced English

READING AND COMPREHENSION

UNIT 9A

Ban plastic straws

1. Say NO to plastic straws. You use them once and then throw them away. Plastic straws last for hundreds of years. They end up in landfill or in the sea or waterways.

2. My big sister likes to snorkel. She told me that last week she found more than two hundred straws in the sea. I was shocked.

3. Sea creatures and sea birds think straws are food and often try to eat them. This can make them ill and sometimes they die.

---

1. How long do plastic straws last?
    A a few years
    B two hundred years
    C hundreds of years

2. Sea creatures often see plastic straws as
    A food.
    B landfill.
    C rubbish.

3. What does the writer think you should say 'NO' to?
    A banning plastic straws
    B using plastic straws
    C snorkelling for plastic straws

4. Are plastic straws good for landfill?
    A No, they take up space for too long.
    B No, there is more room for them in the sea.
    C Yes, they fill it up very quickly.

5. Which statement gives a reason for banning plastic straws?
    A My big sister went snorkelling yesterday.
    B Sea creatures can die from eating plastic straws.
    C Plastic straws make drinking easy.

6. Why is the author 'shocked' (line 8) by what her sister found?

....
....

Answers and explanations on page 110

Excel Advanced Skills: Year 1 Advanced English

UNIT 9B

SPELLING

Write the correct spelling of the underlined words in questions 1–4.

1. I have a big <u>sisster</u>.

2. We think <u>plasstic</u> straws should be banned.

3. Sea <u>creetures</u> need food not straws.

4. I was <u>shokked</u> by the news.

5. Write three words that end with **ie**.

VOCABULARY

6. Circle the word that has the nearest meaning to the underlined word.

    Some sea <u>creatures</u> die from eating plastic.
    - A monsters
    - B animals
    - C giants
    - D things

7. Which word from the text means **don't allow; forbid**?

8. Add a word from the text to the sentence.

    It is a waste to use something only _____.

9. Circle the word that does **not** belong.
    - A sea
    - B ocean
    - C waterway
    - D landfill

GRAMMAR

10. Complete the sentence with a common noun from the text.

    We will not use plastic _____ anymore.

11. Choose a verb or verb group from the box to correctly complete the sentence.

    | thought | thinks | think | was thinking |

    Sea birds _____ straws are for eating.

12. Write words from the text to tell **when**.

    She found two hundred straws _____.

13. Choose a word from the box to correctly complete the sentence.

    | and | so | but | because | or |

    Plastic straws should be banned _____ they harm sea creatures.

PUNCTUATION

Rewrite the sentences correctly.

14. can you snorkel

15. will you stop using plastic straws

Answers and explanations on page 110

UNIT 9C

TEXTS IN CONTEXT

1 **Ban plastic straws**

❶ Say NO to plastic straws. You use them once and then throw them away. Plastic straws last for hundreds of years. They end up in landfill or in the sea or waterways.

❷ My big sister likes to snorkel. She told me that last week she found more than two hundred straws in the sea. I was shocked.

❸ Sea creatures and sea birds think straws are food and often try to eat them. This can make them ill and sometimes they die.

1. This text is about why it is important
   A to ban plastic straws.
   B to put plastic straws in landfill.
   C to learn more about sea creatures.

2. Who is this text written for?
   A everybody
   B young children
   C adults

3. Which paragraph has information that you would **not** find in an encyclopedia?
   A paragraph one
   B paragraph two
   C paragraph three

4. Why is 'NO' (line 2) in capital letters?
   A to help the reader decide what to do
   B to make the 'O' look like the circle in the picture
   C to show the writer thinks saying no is very important

5. The circle with the line through it in the picture means
   A Stop.
   B NO.
   C Please.

6. Does this text make you want plastic straws to be banned? Explain.

   ....
   ....
   ....
   ....

Get creative

7. Create a sign that means no dogs allowed.

Answers and explanations on page 110

READING AND COMPREHENSION

UNIT 10A

Cows

❶ Cows are cattle. A male cow is called a bull, a female is called a cow and a baby is called a calf. Cows mainly eat hay, grasses, corn and alfalfa. They need to drink a lot of water every day. They spend roughly eight hours a day feeding, eight hours chewing their cud and eight hours sleeping.

❷ Most of the milk people drink comes from cows. Farmers use machines to get the milk from the cows' udders. Cows can also be milked by hand. Their milk can be made into cream, cheese, butter and yoghurt.

1. A baby cow is called a
   - A bull.
   - B cow.
   - C calf.

2. Cows need to drink _____ water.
   - A some
   - B a lot of
   - C very little

3. What is yoghurt made from?
   - A milk
   - B udders
   - C grasses

4. How do machines help farmers get milk?
   - A by pumping milk from the cows' udders
   - B by pushing milk into the cows' udders
   - C by spraying the cows' udders

5. Cows spend _____ of time feeding, chewing and sleeping.
   - A the same amount
   - B very different amounts
   - C almost the same amount

6. Which statement is **not** true?
   - A All milk comes from cows.
   - B Most milk comes from cows.
   - C Goats, sheep and yaks can provide milk.

Answers and explanations on page 110

UNIT 10B

SPELLING

Write the correct spelling of the underlined words in questions 1–4.

1. Milk can be turned into <u>creem</u>.

   ....

2. These days many farmers use <u>mashines</u> to milk.

   ....

3. She fed the <u>carf</u> by hand.

   ....

4. You need to grip the <u>uders</u> firmly.

   ....

5. Write three words that rhyme with **ow**.

   ....

VOCABULARY

6. Circle the word that has a similar meaning to the underlined word.

   Cows <u>mainly</u> eat grasses.
   - A mostly
   - B always
   - C sometimes
   - D often

7. Which word from the text means **rechewed food**?

   ....

8. Add a word from the text to the sentence.

   Cows sleep for .... eight hours a day.

9. Circle the word that does **not** belong.
   - A eat
   - B drink
   - C munch
   - D chew

GRAMMAR

10. Complete the sentence with a common noun from the text.

    Farmers often use .... for milking.

11. Choose a verb or verb group from the box to correctly complete the sentence.

    | come | comes | is coming | came |

    Most people know milk .... from cows.

12. Write words from the text to tell **when**.

    Cows need to drink lots of water ....

13. Choose a word from the box to correctly complete the sentence.

    | and | so | but | because | or |

    Males are bulls .... females are cows.

PUNCTUATION

Rewrite the sentences correctly.

14. did you see our newborn calves

    ....

    ....

15. we make cheese cream and butter at our farm

    ....

    ....

    ....

Answers and explanations on page 111

TEXTS IN CONTEXT

UNIT **10C**

Cows

❶ Cows are cattle. A male cow is called a bull, a female is called a cow and a baby is called a calf. Cows mainly eat hay, grasses, corn and alfalfa. They need to drink a lot of water every day. They spend roughly eight hours a day feeding, eight hours chewing their cud and eight hours sleeping.

❷ Most of the milk people drink comes from cows. Farmers use machines to get the milk from the cows' udders. Cows can also be milked by hand. Their milk can be made into cream, cheese, butter and yoghurt.

1. This text is
   A a discussion.
   B a recount.
   C an information report.

2. Where would you find this text?
   A in a book about animals
   B in an ad for milk
   C in a list of things to do

3. What title would suit the second paragraph.
   A Feeding on the farm
   B Cows and their milk
   C The habits of cows

4. The author tells the reader
   A everything there is to know about cows.
   B the most important things to know about cows.
   C some things to know about cows.

5. What do you **not** learn from the words of this text?
   A what cows eat and drink
   B what cows look like
   C how milk is taken from cows

6. This text is made up mainly of
   A facts.
   B arguments.
   C events.

Get creative

7. Take a small, clean bottle with a lid. Add cream until it is three-quarters full. Add a marble and put on the lid. Shake for about fifteen minutes! What's in the bottle now?

Answers and explanations on page 111

READING AND COMPREHENSION

UNIT 11A

Sad the Dog by Sandy Fussell

Our teacher read *Sad the Dog* to us today. It is one of my favourite books. I like the way you get sad for Sad at the start of the book but then you feel glad for him by the end. It is the same with the pictures. Some of them make you laugh but others make you cry. The part I like best is when Sad's new owner, Jack, decides to name his dog Lucky. I have a soft toy at home that looks a bit like the dog in this book. Mum knitted it for me.

by Melanie

1. Who read the book *Sad the Dog* to the class?
   A Melanie
   B Jack
   C the teacher

2. When was the book read to the class?
   A yesterday
   B today
   C tomorrow

3. Who does Melanie's soft toy look a bit like?
   A a dog
   B Sad the dog
   C Jack

4. Had Melanie heard this book before?
   A yes
   B no
   C maybe

5. What changes Sad's life?
   A having a soft toy made like him
   B having Melanie like him
   C having Jack as his owner

6. The book is a favourite with Melanie because
   A she has a soft toy like Sad.
   B she likes how it makes her feel.
   C she likes dogs.

Answers and explanations on page 111

Excel Advanced Skills: Year 1 Advanced English

UNIT 11B

SPELLING

Write the correct spelling of the underlined words in questions 1–4.

1. We had a really good story <u>tooday</u>.

   ....

2. Books that make you <u>larf</u> are good fun.

   ....

3. Jack is Sad's new <u>oner</u>.

   ....

4. I have a <u>nitted</u> dog at home.

   ....

5. Write three words that end with **ad**.

   ....

   ....

VOCABULARY

6. Circle the word that has a similar meaning to the underlined word.

   That's the part I like <u>best</u>.
   - A better
   - B most
   - C more
   - D good

7. Which word from the text means **owned by me**?

   ....

8. Add a word from the text to the sentence.

   Some of the pictures made me .... and some made me cry!

9. Circle the word that does **not** belong.
   - A sad
   - B sorry
   - C glad
   - D gloomy

GRAMMAR

10. Complete the sentence with a common noun from the text.

    It is one of my favourite ....

11. Choose a verb from the box to correctly complete the sentence.

    | knits | knitting | knit | knitted |

    Mum .... a toy dog for me to play with.

12. Write words from the text to tell **when**.

    I felt glad for Sad ....

    .... of the book.

13. Choose a word from the box to correctly complete the sentence.

    | and | so | but | because | or |

    I liked the book .... it did make me sad.

PUNCTUATION

Rewrite the sentences correctly.

14. what is your favourite book

    ....

    ....

15. has tom read this book yet

    ....

    ....

Answers and explanations on page 111

UNIT 11C

TEXTS IN CONTEXT

1 **Sad the Dog by Sandy Fussell**

2 Our teacher read *Sad the Dog* to us
3 today. It is one of my favourite books.
4 I like the way you get sad for Sad at
5 the start of the book but then you feel
6 glad for him by the end. It is the same
7 with the pictures. Some of them make
8 you laugh but others make you cry.
9 The part I like best is when Sad's new
10 owner, Jack, decides to name his dog
11 Lucky. I have a soft toy at home that
12 looks a bit like the dog in this book.
13 Mum knitted it for me.

14 by Melanie

1 This text tells
   A the story of a book.
   B what Melanie thinks about a book.
   C why Melanie's mum made her a soft toy.

2 This text would be helpful for someone
   A wanting to learn how to look after a dog.
   B looking for a good book to read.
   C learning how to knit a toy dog.

3 The reasons Melanie likes the book can be found in _____ of the text.
   A the middle section
   B the first two sentences
   C the last two sentences

4 In line 4, why does the first 'sad' not have a capital letter but the next 'Sad' does?
   A The first is the name of the dog; the second describes a feeling.
   B Melanie made a mistake. They should both be capital letters.
   C The first describes a feeling; the second is the name of the dog.

5 Another title for this text could be
   A Jack's favourite book.
   B Melanie's favourite book.
   C Jack's favourite dog.

6 Do you think you would like the book *Sad the Dog*? Why or why not?

   ....
   ....
   ....
   ....

Get creative

7 Write down the name of your favourite book. Write a sentence about why you like it.

👉 Answers and explanations on page 111

Excel Advanced Skills: Year 1 Advanced English

READING AND COMPREHENSION

UNIT 12A

Bees

❶ Bees visit plants to feed on nectar and pollen. They fly between plants and carry pollen from one plant to another. This means new flowers, fruits and vegetables are able to grow. Bees in our gardens help this happen.

❷ How can we help the bees? Don't use harmful sprays at any time. Have plants in your garden that provide food for bees such as lavender. Bees need water too. Leave out a bowl of clean, shallow water for them. It helps to add a small rock so they can land there when they come to drink.

1. Why do bees visit plants?
   A to feed
   B to carry pollen
   C to grow flowers

2. What do bees need as well as nectar and pollen?
   A rock
   B harmful sprays
   C water

3. Which plants do bees visit?
   A all plants
   B plants that have nectar
   C all trees

4. How do bees help new plants to form?
   A by carrying pollen from one plant to another
   B by drinking the nectar of plants
   C by sipping water

5. Which action could harm the bees?
   A leaving clean water for them
   B using sprays
   C planting lavender

6. Why is it important to care for bees? Explain. ....

....

☞ Answers and explanations on page 111

Excel Advanced Skills: Year 1 Advanced English

UNIT 12B

SPELLING

Write the correct spelling of the underlined words in questions 1–4.

1. We get lots of bees in our <u>guarden</u>.

2. It is good to leave out some <u>warter</u> for them.

3. Harmful <u>spraiys</u> can kill bees.

4. Bees spread <u>polen</u> from one plant to another.

5. Write three words that end with **oo**.

VOCABULARY

6. Circle the word that has a similar meaning to the underlined word.

   There are some ways we can <u>assist</u> bees to do their good work.
   - A make
   - B force
   - C push
   - D help

7. Which word from the text means **not very deep**?

8. Add a word from the text to the sentence.

   Plants _____ nectar for bees.

9. Circle the word that does **not** belong.
   - A helpful
   - B useful
   - C harmful
   - D safe

GRAMMAR

10. Complete the sentence with a common noun from the text.

    We need bees in our _____.

11. Choose a verb from the box to correctly complete the sentence.

    | carry | carried | carries | carrying |

    Bees _____ pollen from one plant to another.

12. Write words from the text to tell **when**.

    Harmful sprays should not be used _____.

13. Choose a word from the box to correctly complete the sentence.

    | and | so | but | because | or |

    Bees visit plants _____ they can gather nectar from them.

PUNCTUATION

Rewrite the sentences correctly.

14. do you have bees in your garden

15. we grow flowers fruit and vegetables

Answers and explanations on pages 111–112

Excel Advanced Skills: Year 1 Advanced English

TEXTS IN CONTEXT

UNIT 12C

Bees

1
2 ❶ Bees visit plants to feed on nectar and
3   pollen. They fly between plants and carry
4   pollen from one plant to another. This
5   means new flowers, fruits and vegetables
6   are able to grow. Bees in our gardens help
7   this happen.

8 ❷ How can we help the bees? Don't use
9   harmful sprays at any time. Have plants in
10   your garden that provide food for bees such
11   as lavender. Bees need water too. Leave
12   out a bowl of clean, shallow water for
13   them. It helps to add a small rock so they
14   can land there when they come to drink.

1 Where would you **not** find this text?
   A on a web page about bees
   B in a book about gardening
   C in a diary

2 The text is made up mainly of
   A facts.
   B arguments.
   C questions.

3 Paragraph two lists
   A when to help bees.
   B advice about helping bees.
   C events in the lives of bees.

4 How many ways to help bees are listed in the text?
   A two   B three   C four

5 What are the bees doing in the picture?

   ....

   ....

6 What else might carry pollen from plant to plant?

   ....

   ....

   ....

Get creative

7 Find out the answers to these questions.

   Is it true that some people are allergic to bee stings?

   What happens to a bee after it stings?

☞ Answers and explanations on page 112

45

Excel Advanced Skills: Year 1 Advanced English

READING AND COMPREHENSION

UNIT 13A

1 **The Glower**

2 And that's the news to the minute. [The news ends and the screen
3 crosses to the picture below.]

4 Have you ever seen such glowing teeth? Would you like yours to look
5 just like Bill's in the picture? Glowing with health? Glowing with shine?
6 Well, YOU are in luck.

7 All you need is The Glower and The Glower is in the shops now. Fresh
8 on the market.

9 The Glower is a toothpaste that will
10 change your teeth—and your life—forever.
11 Get The Glower right now. You won't look
12 back. You'll be glowing—the envy of
13 everyone.

1 What is The Glower?
   A teeth
   B toothpaste
   C a boy named Bill

2 Whose teeth can you see in the picture?
   A Bill's
   B a cartoon character's
   C a shopkeeper's

3 What will change if you use The Glower?
   A your teeth
   B your life
   C your teeth and your life

4 'Fresh on the market' (lines 7–8) means
   A you can buy it online.
   B the writer found some at a market.
   C it is on sale for the first time.

5 Do Bill's teeth look as if they are glowing with health and shine?
   A yes
   B not really
   C almost

6 Would you buy The Glower? Why or why not?

....

....

Answers and explanations on page 112

UNIT 13B

SPELLING

Write the correct spelling of the underlined words in questions 1–4.

1. My teeth already glow with <u>helth</u>!

   _____

2. What <u>toothpaiste</u> do you use?

   _____

3. <u>Everywon</u> wants some.

   _____

4. You can buy it <u>rite</u> now.

   _____

5. Write three words that end with **op**.

   _____
   _____

VOCABULARY

6. Circle the answer that has the nearest meaning to the underlined words.

   It is the toothpaste that will <u>change</u> your life.
   - A break
   - B shift
   - C make
   - D alter

7. Which word from the text means **brightness or gloss**?

   _____

8. Add a word from the text to the sentence.

   Everyone wants teeth that are _____ with health.

9. Circle the word that does **not** belong.
   - A everybody
   - B everyone
   - C people
   - D nobody

GRAMMAR

10. Complete the sentence with a common noun from the text.

    Don't you want your _____ to shine?

11. Choose a verb or verb group from the box to correctly complete the sentence.

    | is | are | will be | being |

    The Glower _____ fresh on the market.

12. Write words from the text to tell **when**.

    You should buy The Glower _____.

13. Choose a word from the box to correctly complete the sentence.

    | and | so | but | because | or |

    I will buy The Glower _____ I want to have shiny teeth.

PUNCTUATION

Rewrite the sentences correctly.

14. have you bought yours yet

    _____
    _____

15. dont you like bills smile

    _____
    _____

TEXTS IN CONTEXT

UNIT 13C

1 **The Glower**

2 And that's the news to the minute. [The news ends and the screen
3 crosses to the picture below.]

4 Have you ever seen such glowing teeth? Would you like yours to look
5 just like Bill's in the picture? Glowing with health? Glowing with shine?
6 Well, YOU are in luck.

7 All you need is The Glower and The Glower is in the shops now. Fresh
8 on the market.

9 The Glower is a toothpaste that will
10 change your teeth—and your life—forever.
11 Get The Glower right now. You won't look
12 back. You'll be glowing—the envy of
13 everyone.

1. The purpose of this text is to
   A sell a product.
   B recount events.
   C tell a story.

2. This text is spoken
   A on the radio.
   B on television.
   C in a book.

3. Why is 'YOU' (line 6) in capital letters?
   A to make the viewer seem important
   B to make the viewer seem unimportant
   C to show the viewer who it refers to

4. The text aims to make viewers .... people who use The Glower.
   A envy
   B dislike
   C like

5. The claims made for what The Glower can do for you
   A are ridiculous.
   B are likely to happen.
   C could probably happen.

6. How does the picture relate to the text?

   ....
   ....
   ....
   ....

Get creative

7. What advertisements catch your interest? Explain.

Answers and explanations on page 112

48

Excel Advanced Skills: Year 1 Advanced English

READING AND COMPREHENSION

UNIT 14A

Crows

❶ Crows are birds whose feathers are glossy and black. They like to live in open areas with trees and water nearby. They also live happily in cities and suburbs. They eat most things including small animals, insects and worms.

❷ Crows are very good at giving information to each other. Their cries are loud and get even louder when they chat together.

❸ They are very clever birds. They have good memories. They don't forget faces and they can find food they have hidden months earlier. They crack shellfish and nuts on rocks to open them. They can also find objects to use as tools to get food or build nests.

1. What colour are crows' feathers?
   - A glossy
   - B black
   - C white

2. What do crows crack shellfish and nuts on?
   - A water
   - B food
   - C rocks

3. Crows are _____ birds.
   - A friendly
   - B clever
   - C hungry

4. Crows can't live without
   - A small animals.
   - B insects.
   - C water.

5. When would crows need a good memory?
   - A when food is scarce
   - B when they are hurt
   - C when they are opening shellfish

6. What is the cleverest thing crows do? Explain.

Answers and explanations on page 112

Excel Advanced Skills: Year 1 Advanced English

UNIT 14B

SPELLING

Write the correct spelling of the underlined words in questions 1–4.

1. Crows' <u>fethers</u> are very shiny.

   ....

2. Crows talk to <u>eech</u> other.

   ....

3. Crows have good <u>memmories</u>.

   ....

4. Crows pass <u>infawmation</u> to other crows.

   ....

5. Write three words that end with **et**.

   ....

   ....

VOCABULARY

6. Circle the word that has a similar meaning to the underlined word.

   Crows live <u>happily</u> in cities.
   - A unhappily
   - B uneasily
   - C contentedly
   - D unwillingly

7. Which word from the text means **close at hand; not far off?**

   ....

8. Add a word from the text to the sentence.

   Crows, like humans, use .... to help them get food.

9. Circle the word that does **not** belong.
   - A forget
   - B recollect
   - C recall
   - D remember

GRAMMAR

10. Complete the sentence with a common noun from the text.

    Crows have glossy, black ....

11. Choose a verb or verb group from the box to correctly complete the sentence.

    | had | have had | are having | have |

    These birds .... very good memories.

12. Write words from the text to tell **when**.

    Mr Crow got the food he had hidden ....

13. Choose a word from the box to correctly complete the sentence.

    | and | so | but | because | or |

    Crows are clever .... they have good memories.

PUNCTUATION

Rewrite the sentences correctly.

14. she saw the crow pick up the worm

    ....

    ....

15. are there crows where you live

    ....

    ....

Answers and explanations on pages 112–113

TEXTS IN CONTEXT

UNIT **14C**

Crows

1. Crows are birds whose feathers are glossy and black. They like to live in open areas with trees and water nearby. They also live happily in cities and suburbs. They eat most things including small animals, insects and worms.

2. Crows are very good at giving information to each other. Their cries are loud and get even louder when they chat together.

3. They are very clever birds. They have good memories. They don't forget faces and they can find food they have hidden months earlier. They crack shellfish and nuts on rocks to open them. They can also find objects to use as tools to get food or build nests.

1. The purpose of this text is to
   A persuade.
   B retell events.
   C give information.

2. Where would you find this text?
   A in a school magazine.
   B in a book about birds.
   C in a fairytale.

3. Sometimes crows steal windscreen wiper rubbers to line their nests.

   To which paragraph could this sentence be added?
   A paragraph one
   B paragraph two
   C paragraph three

4. What is **not** included in this text?
   A how crows sound
   B how crows care for their young
   C what crows eat

5. The use of the word 'chat' (line 10) makes crows sound like
   A friendly human beings.
   B noisy birds
   C silly chatterboxes.

6. The writer suggests crows are
   .... birds.
   A shy
   B bold
   C cheerful

Get creative

7. Write down what you think the crows are saying to each other in the picture.

Answers and explanations on page 113

READING AND COMPREHENSION

UNIT 15A

The surprise

"Maybe in a year or so, Bobby," said Mum when I asked her. "Perhaps a bit later," said Dad when I asked him. I really want a kitten!

*****

Dear Diary

Today is my sixth birthday. Mum and Dad have changed their minds. My present is a kitten! It has brown and white fur. It is the softest fur I've ever felt.

I'm going to take the best care of my kitten.
I will teach it to use the kitty litter tray.
I'll wash its food dishes every day.
We'll play games together.

"What shall I call you, little kitten?" "Meow," it replied.

1. It is Bobby's _____ birthday.
   A fourth
   B fifth
   C sixth

2. What colour is Bobby's kitten
   A brown
   B brown and white
   C white

3. Who did Bobby ask for a kitten?
   A his mum and dad
   B his mum
   C his dad

4. Why doesn't the kitten have a name?
   A It is already called Bobby.
   B Bobby hasn't chosen a name yet.
   C Mum and Dad have forgotten what it is.

5. When the kitten says "Meow" it is most likely
   A 'talking' to Bobby in cat talk.
   B telling Bobby to name it Meow.
   C showing Bobby it is scared.

6. Do you think Bobby will do all the things he plans? _____

Answers and explanations on page 113

UNIT 15B

SPELLING

Write the correct spelling of the underlined words in questions 1–4.

1. When is your <u>sickth</u> birthday?

   ....

2. What was your birthday <u>pressent</u>?

   ....

3. I have a new <u>kiten</u>!

   ....

4. It has brown and white <u>furr</u>.

   ....

5. Write three words that end with **um**.

   ....

   ....

VOCABULARY

6. Circle the word that has a similar meaning to the underlined word.

   You can't have that until <u>later</u>.
   - A soon
   - B before
   - C afterwards
   - D earlier

7. Which word from the text means **maybe**?

   ....

8. Add a word from the text to the sentence.

   I'll try my .... to look after my cat.

9. Circle the word that does **not** belong.
   - A perhaps
   - B maybe
   - C possibly
   - D clearly

GRAMMAR

10. Complete the sentence with a common noun from the text.

    Does your cat use the kitty litter .... yet?

11. Choose a verb from the box to correctly complete the sentence.

    | teaches | taught | teach | teaching |

    I plan to .... my kitten lots of things.

12. Write words from the text to tell **when**.

    I'll take care of my kitten ....

    ....

13. Choose a word from the box to correctly complete the sentence.

    | and | so | but | because | or |

    I'll keep my kitten clean .... it will stay healthy.

PUNCTUATION

Rewrite the sentences correctly.

14. have you seen my kitten

    ....

    ....

15. i think bobby will love his kitten

    ....

    ....

    ....

Answers and explanations on page 113

53

TEXTS IN CONTEXT

UNIT **15C**

1 **The surprise**

2 "Maybe in a year or so, Bobby," said Mum when I asked her. "Perhaps
3 a bit later," said Dad when I asked him. I really want a kitten!

*****

4 Dear Diary

5 Today is my sixth birthday. Mum and Dad have changed
6 their minds. My present is a kitten! It has brown
7 and white fur. It is the softest fur I've ever felt.

8 I'm going to take the best care of my kitten.
9 I will teach it to use the kitty litter tray.
10 I'll wash its food dishes every day.
11 We'll play games together.

12 "What shall I call you, little kitten?" "Meow," it replied.

---

1. The first paragraph includes
   A reports of what Mum and Dad said.
   B descriptions of what Mum and Dad look like.
   C conversations about Mum and Dad.

2. The part beginning 'Dear Diary' records the thoughts of
   A Mum.
   B Dad.
   C Bobby.

3. The first paragraph happened .... the diary entry.
   A before
   B at the same time as
   C after

4. What is the exclamation mark used for (line 6)?
   A to express surprise
   B to express strong feelings
   C to give a command

5. How does Bobby speak to his kitten?
   A gently
   B roughly
   C unhappily

6. How well does the picture suit the text? Explain.

   ....
   ....
   ....

Get creative

7. What name do you think would suit the kitten? Why?

☞ Answers and explanations on page 113

54

Excel Advanced Skills: Year 1 Advanced English

NAPLAN-style Reading Test 2

Kookaburras

Kookaburras are birds. They like to eat insects, lizards and snakes. They often dive down from a branch to catch a tasty worm. Do you know the song 'Kookaburra sits in the old gum tree'?

You may have heard kookaburras laughing in the bush or in your garden at home. They don't really laugh but their call sounds like a rather loud laugh. Their favourite time to 'laugh' is at dawn and then at dusk. (Dawn is early in the morning and dusk is just before evening.) People in the bush sometimes use them as a clock! Their numbers have declined for numerous reasons including the spread of housing, logging, back-burning and large bushfires.

---

1. Where does the kookaburra sit in the song?
   - A in the bush
   - B in the morning
   - C in the old gum tree

2. When do kookaburras most like to make their call?
   - A at dawn
   - B at dusk
   - C at dawn and dusk

3. When is dusk?
   - A in the early morning
   - B in the early evening
   - C in the night-time

4. Which statement is true?
   - A Kookaburras often dive down to catch their food.
   - B Kookaburras won't go near snakes.
   - C Kookaburras always laugh softly.

5. What is the purpose of the text?
   - A to teach you how to look after kookaburras
   - B to tell a story about kookaburras
   - C to give information about kookaburras

6. Kookaburras are used as clocks because they call
   - A whenever they feel like it.
   - B at the same time each day.
   - C when they find food.

7. Why are brackets used in lines 9–11?
   - A The sentence belongs to a different text.
   - B The sentence isn't directly about kookaburras.
   - C The sentence belongs at the end of the text.

Answers and explanations on page 113

Excel Advanced Skills: **Year 1 Advanced English**

NAPLAN-style Conventions of Language Test 2

The spelling mistakes in these sentences have been underlined. Write the correct spelling on the lines.

1. They put <u>there</u> books in their bags.

2. <u>Everyboddy</u> was at my party!

3. We had toast and <u>hunney</u> for breakfast.

4. My <u>pairents</u> are coming to our play.

5. Are you in Year One at <u>skool</u>?

Read the text. Choose the correct word to complete the sentences.

> We are _____(6)_____ the beach and it is already very hot. Mum says we have to swim _____(7)_____ the flags where we will be safe. I can't wait to _____(8)_____ into the water to cool off.

6. A in   B over
   C at   D with

7. A across   B between
   C beneath   D under

8. A got   B getting
   C gets   D get

9. Which word is a common noun in the sentence?

   You have got mud all over you now!

   A You   B got
   C mud   D now.

10. Complete this sentence with the correct word.

    When we went to the beach it _____ cold and windy.

    A was
    B is
    C are
    D were

11. Which words tell **when**?

    We learned how to play games on the computer after school.

    A We learned
    B how to play games
    C on the computer
    D after school

12. Which word correctly completes the sentence?

    Do you want jam _____ would you rather have honey on your toast?

    A and
    B but
    C or
    D so

13. Which sentence is punctuated correctly?
    A please answer when I ask you a question.
    B Please answer when I ask you a question
    C Please answer when I ask you a question?
    D Please answer when I ask you a question.

14. Which sentence is punctuated correctly?
    A Will Dad read me a story before I go to sleep?
    B Will Dad read me a story before I go to sleep.
    C Will Dad read me a story before I go to sleep!
    D will dad read me a story before I go to sleep?

Answers and explanations on page 113

READING AND COMPREHENSION

UNIT 16A

GOOD NEWS

❶ Some time ago, a giraffe named Kitoto was taken on a very long road trip across Australia. She was taken safely from the Sydney zoo to the Perth zoo. The plan was for her to meet a giraffe named Armani.

❷ Now they have a baby giraffe. The baby is about 160 cm tall and is a bit wobbly on her feet. She will need to drink Kitoto's milk for about a year. There is a competition for people to choose the baby a name.

❸ This is a good news story because we need more giraffes. We don't want them to die out. Well done!

1. Where was Kitoto taken?
   - A Sydney
   - B Perth
   - C Armani

2. How did she travel?
   - A by road
   - B by sea
   - C by air

3. The baby
   - A is called Armani.
   - B is called Kitoto.
   - C doesn't have a name yet.

4. You can tell she is a baby because
   - A she drinks her mother's milk.
   - B she is a female giraffe.
   - C she doesn't have a name.

5. Which statement is **not** true?
   - A Baby giraffes drink milk from their mothers.
   - B Giraffes must go on road trips to have their babies.
   - C People don't want giraffes to die out.

6. Does the writer think that giraffes could die out?
   - A yes
   - B no
   - C maybe

👉 Answers and explanations on pages 113–114

Excel Advanced Skills: Year 1 Advanced English

UNIT 16B

SPELLING

Write the correct spelling of the underlined words in questions 1–4.

1. I saw a <u>girrafe</u> at the zoo.

   ....

2. Have you ever been on a <u>rode</u> trip?

   ....

3. The baby was <u>wobblie</u> on its feet.

   ....

4. What name would you <u>chooze</u>?

   ....

5. Change the first letter of **will** to make three rhyming words.

   ....

VOCABULARY

6. Circle the word that has a similar meaning to the underlined word.

   It was a <u>long</u> trip.
   - **A** high
   - **B** tall
   - **C** lengthy
   - **D** faraway

7. Which word from the text means **a contest**?

   ....

8. Add a word from the text to the sentence.

   She went from east to west .... Australia.

9. Circle the word that does **not** belong.
   - **A** more
   - **B** fewer
   - **C** less
   - **D** none

GRAMMAR

10. Complete the sentence with a proper noun from the text.

    I saw a giraffe called .... in the zoo.

11. Choose a verb or verb group from the box to correctly complete the sentence.

    | are | will be | is | were |

    The baby giraffe .... unsteady on her feet.

12. Write a word from the text to tell **how**.

    Kitoto was taken ....

    .... from Sydney to Perth.

13. Choose a pronoun from the box to correctly complete the sentence.

    | he | she | it | you | they | I | we |

    Kitoto loves her baby and .... feeds it with her milk.

PUNCTUATION

Rewrite the sentences correctly.

14. well done kitoto

    ....

    ....

15. thats wonderful news

    ....

    ....

Answers and explanations on page 114

TEXTS IN CONTEXT

UNIT 16C

GOOD NEWS

❶ Some time ago, a giraffe named Kitoto was taken on a very long road trip across Australia. She was taken safely from the Sydney zoo to the Perth zoo. The plan was for her to meet a giraffe named Armani.

❷ Now they have a baby giraffe. The baby is about 160 cm tall and is a bit wobbly on her feet. She will need to drink Kitoto's milk for about a year. There is a competition for people to choose the baby a name.

❸ This is a good news story because we need more giraffes. We don't want them to die out. Well done!

1. This text is about
   A   the habits of giraffes.
   B   a new-born giraffe in a Perth zoo.
   C   how giraffes get their names.

2. You would find this text in
   A   a book about animals.
   B   a newspaper.
   C   a dictionary.

3. The first paragraph tells the reader
   A   why Kitoto was taken to the Perth zoo.
   B   why more giraffes are needed.
   C   why this is a good news story.

4. The picture is closely linked to paragraph
   A   one.
   B   two.
   C   three.

5. Another title for the text could be
   A   Name the giraffe.
   B   Why you need to visit a zoo near you.
   C   Baby giraffe born in zoo.

6. Why do you think there is a competition to choose a name for the baby?

   ....

   ....

   ....

Get creative

7. Find two more facts about baby giraffes.

Answers and explanations on page 114

READING AND COMPREHENSION

UNIT 17A

Yoda

My name is Yoda. I am learning to be a guide dog. I am the dog on the right in the photo. I live with the Monroe family. They all look after me. Dad takes me to training and Mum, Sal and Hen take me for walks every day. I have been living with them for nearly a year now.

Soon I will be ready to leave and live with a new family. I will miss the Monroes badly but I'm looking forward to being a real guide dog. Then I will be able to look after someone who can't see.

1. Yoda is the name of
   - A a person.
   - B a guide.
   - C a dog.

2. Guide dogs look after people who can't
   - A walk well.
   - B see well.
   - C hear well.

3. Yoda lives with
   - A Sal and Hen.
   - B Mum and Dad.
   - C the Monroe family.

4. How long does it take to learn to be a guide dog?
   - A less than a year
   - B much more than a year
   - C about a year

5. What will make leaving the Monroes feel not so bad?
   - A living with a new family
   - B helping someone who can't see well
   - C going for walks in a new place

6. Will Yoda make a good guide dog? Why or why not?

Answers and explanations on page 114

Excel Advanced Skills: Year 1 Advanced English

UNIT 17B

SPELLING

Write the correct spelling of the underlined words in questions 1–4.

1. My friend has a <u>giude</u> dog.

2. I've lived with them for <u>neerly</u> a year now.

3. Dad knows <u>somewon</u> who trains dogs.

4. Are you <u>abel</u> to take the dog for a walk?

5. Change the first letter of **look** to make three rhyming words.

VOCABULARY

6. Circle the word that has a similar meaning to the underlined word.

   <u>Nearly</u> a year has gone by already.
   - A Exactly
   - B Lately
   - C Now
   - D Almost

7. Which word from the text means **help someone find their way**?

8. Add a word from the text to the sentence.

   The black dog is on the left but I am on the _____.

9. Circle the word that does **not** belong.
   - A learn
   - B teach
   - C train
   - D coach

GRAMMAR

10. Complete the sentence with a proper noun from the text.

    Yoda lives with the _____.

11. Choose a verb from the box to correctly complete the sentence.

    | am | are | were | is |

    I _____ going to live with a new family soon.

12. Write words from the text to tell **how**.

    I'm going to miss the family _____.

13. Choose a pronoun from the box to correctly complete the sentence.

    | he | she | it | you | they | I | we |

    I will miss Sal and Hen because _____ play with me.

PUNCTUATION

Rewrite the sentences correctly.

14. im so excited

15. they take me for a walk every day

Answers and explanations on page 114

61

Excel Advanced Skills: Year 1 Advanced English

UNIT 17C

TEXTS IN CONTEXT

1 **Yoda**

2 My name is Yoda. I am learning to be a guide dog. I am the dog on the
3 right in the photo. I live with the Monroe family. They all look after me.
4 Dad takes me to training and Mum, Sal and Hen take me for walks
5 every day. I have been living with them for nearly a year now.

6 Soon I will be ready to leave and live with a new family. I will miss the
7 Monroes badly but I'm looking forward to being a real guide dog.
8 Then I will be able to look after someone who can't see.

1. The text is about
   A what Yoda's family thinks about her.
   B a day in the life of Yoda.
   C what Yoda feels about things.

2. The text helps you get to know Yoda because it is told
   A by her.
   B by her new family.
   C by Mr Monroe.

3. Where could the sentence 'I can't wait!' be added?
   A in a new paragraph at the beginning
   B in the middle of the first paragraph
   C at the end of the second paragraph

4. Another title for this text could be
   A The Monroes.
   B Learning to be a guide dog.
   C Yoda's two families.

5. How would Yoda describe the Monroe family?
   A caring
   B strict
   C careless

6. What does the picture tell you about Yoda that is not in the text?

   ....

   ....

Get creative

7. Imagine you are someone's pet. Write about your thoughts and feelings.

Answers and explanations on page 114

62

Excel Advanced Skills: Year 1 Advanced English

READING AND COMPREHENSION

UNIT 18A

1 **Aussie Rules**

2 Aussie Rules is the name of a type of football played in Australia. It is
3 played with an oval ball on an oval-shaped field. There are two teams
4 who try to win points. Each kick that goes through the goalposts
5 earns six points. If the kick goes between the posts on each side of the
6 goalposts then one point is scored. The game used to be played only
7 by men but now there are women's teams too.

8 Many Indigenous Australians have played skilfully
9 and been stars of the game. Each year,
10 one round (there are 23 rounds before
11 the finals) celebrates these players and
12 their lives. The teams wear special
13 jerseys that tell the stories of Indigenous
14 Australian players.

1. What shape is the football used in Aussie Rules?
   - A square
   - B circular
   - C oval

2. How many points does a goal score?
   - A six
   - B three
   - C one

3. Do women play Aussie Rules?
   - A yes
   - B no
   - C maybe

4. Which statement is **not** true?
   - A The team with the highest score wins.
   - B Aussie rules is a team game.
   - C It is better to kick a point than a goal.

5. How many posts are there at each end of the field?
   - A two
   - B four
   - C six

6. What would you need to do on the field to be called a 'star' (line 9) of the game?

Answers and explanations on page 114

Excel Advanced Skills: Year 1 Advanced English

UNIT 18B

SPELLING

Write the correct spelling of the underlined words in questions 1–4.

1. How many <u>teems</u> are there?

2. She kicked a <u>gaol</u>!

3. It is a very <u>speshial</u> round.

4. Did you know there are <u>woman's</u> teams now?

5. Change the first letter of **game** to make three rhyming words.

VOCABULARY

6. Circle the word that has a similar meaning to the underlined word.

   Rosie and I play for different football <u>teams</u>.
   - A sides
   - B flocks
   - C gangs
   - D troops

7. Which word from the text means **more important than others**?

8. Add a word from the text to the sentence.

   The round celebrates Indigenous Australian _____ and all they have done for the game.

9. Circle the word that does **not** belong.
   - A suns
   - B stars
   - C heroes
   - D planets

GRAMMAR

10. Complete the sentence with a proper noun from the text.

    Aussie Rules is a football game played in _____.

11. Choose a verb or verb group from the box to correctly complete the sentence.

    | wears | wore | is wearing | has worn |

    He _____ his special jersey yesterday in Round 11.

12. Write words from the text to tell **how**.

    They became famous because they played _____.

13. Choose a pronoun from the box to correctly complete the sentence.

    | he | she | it | you | they | I | we |

    Rosie is pleased because _____ is playing in the team this week.

PUNCTUATION

Rewrite the sentences correctly.

14. our team kicked ten goals today

15. i asked my friend to play aussie rules with me

Answers and explanations on page 115

64

Excel Advanced Skills: Year 1 Advanced English

TEXTS IN CONTEXT

UNIT 18C

1 **Aussie Rules**

2 Aussie Rules is the name of a type of football played in Australia. It is
3 played with an oval ball on an oval-shaped field. There are two teams
4 who try to win points. Each kick that goes through the goalposts
5 earns six points. If the kick goes between the posts on each side of the
6 goalposts then one point is scored. The game used to be played only
7 by men but now there are women's teams too.

8 Many Indigenous Australians have played skilfully
9 and been stars of the game. Each year,
10 one round (there are 23 rounds before
11 the finals) celebrates these players and
12 their lives. The teams wear special
13 jerseys that tell the stories of Indigenous
14 Australian players.

1. The first paragraph gives information about
   A the rules of the game.
   B the teams who play the game.
   C different types of games played in Australia.

2. The second paragraph gives information about
   A the rules of the game.
   B a special round in the game.
   C football players.

3. Where could information about the teams' mascots be added?
   A in the first paragraph
   B in the second paragraph
   C in a new paragraph

4. The word 'Aussie' is slang for the word
   A Australia.
   B Australian.
   C Ozzie.

5. Players are described as 'stars' (line 9) when they
   A outshine other players.
   B wear the special jersey.
   C are Indigenous.

6. Do you like playing team games? Why or why not?

Get creative

7. Draw the outline of a jersey on a large piece of paper. Decorate it with words and images that tell the story of your life.

Answers and explanations on page 115

Excel Advanced Skills: Year 1 Advanced English

65

READING AND COMPREHENSION

UNIT 19A

1 **Games to eat**

2 Most board games have a board,
3 counters of some kind and dice.
4 Nothing to eat there. Now an Australian
5 inventor is making some new games
6 that you CAN eat easily. Every little bit
7 of them—even the board!

Playing Veggieland
Photo courtesy of Jenn Sandercock

8 You might have to buy food from the supermarket; or perhaps you
9 will need to do some cooking the night before you play. The names
10 of the games will give you a hint about what you will need to buy:
11 Chocolateland, Cheeseland and Veggieland, for example. There are
12 exciting rules for each game. Do you like this inventor's idea?

1. Dice are used in _____ board games.
   - **A** some
   - **B** no
   - **C** most

2. When might you need to do your cooking?
   - **A** the day of the game
   - **B** the night after the game
   - **C** the night before the game

3. What gives you a hint about what to buy?
   - **A** your shopping list
   - **B** the names of the games
   - **C** the inventor's idea

4. The rules for these new games are
   - **A** different for each game.
   - **B** mostly the same.
   - **C** all the same.

5. What is unusual about these new games?
   - **A** You invent them.
   - **B** You can play them.
   - **C** You can eat them.

6. Would you like to play a game you can eat? Why or why not?

   ....

   ....

Answers and explanations on page 115

Excel Advanced Skills: Year 1 Advanced English

UNIT 19B

SPELLING

Write the correct spelling of the underlined words in questions 1–4.

1. We <u>mite</u> play that game tonight.

   ....

2. The inventor is <u>Austrailian</u>.

   ....

3. Did you buy this at the <u>soopermarket</u>?

   ....

4. I like playing <u>bored</u> games with my friends.

   ....

5. Change the first letter of **kind** to make three rhyming words.

   ....

   ....

VOCABULARY

6. Circle the word that has a similar meaning to the underlined word.

   What did you <u>buy</u> at the supermarket?
   - A purchase
   - B sell
   - C find
   - D get

7. Which word from the text means **a thought or picture in your mind**?

   ....

8. Add a word from the text to the sentence.

   Snakes and Ladders is a game you play on a ....

9. Circle the word that does **not** belong.
   - A author
   - B creator
   - C copycat
   - D inventor

GRAMMAR

10. Complete the sentence with a proper noun from the text.

    .... sounds like a game I'd like as I love chocolate!

11. Choose a verb from the box to correctly complete the sentence.

    | is | are | was | were |

    There .... different rules for each new game.

12. Write a word from the text to tell **how**.

    We ate the whole game ....

13. Choose a pronoun from the box to correctly complete the sentence.

    | he | she | it | you | they | I | we |

    The dice were made of chocolate and .... were yummy to eat.

PUNCTUATION

Rewrite the sentences correctly.

14. you can even eat the board

    ....

    ....

15. what did the dice taste like

    ....

    ....

Answers and explanations on page 115

Excel Advanced Skills: Year 1 Advanced English

TEXTS IN CONTEXT

UNIT 19C

1 **Games to eat**

2 Most board games have a board,
3 counters of some kind and dice.
4 Nothing to eat there. Now an Australian
5 inventor is making some new games
6 that you CAN eat easily. Every little bit
7 of them—even the board!

Playing Veggieland
Photo courtesy of Jenn Sandercock

8 You might have to buy food from the supermarket; or perhaps you
9 will need to do some cooking the night before you play. The names
10 of the games will give you a hint about what you will need to buy:
11 Chocolateland, Cheeseland and Veggieland, for example. There are
12 exciting rules for each game. Do you like this inventor's idea?

1 The purpose of this text is to tell about
   A games.
   B food.
   C a new idea.

2 Where would you **not** find this text?
   A in a magazine
   B on a noticeboard
   C in a newspaper

3 The last sentence is asking for the
   A reader's opinion.
   B inventor's opinion.
   C author's opinion.

4 The exclamation mark (line 7) expresses
   A anger.
   B surprise.
   C sadness.

5 Was Snakes and Ladders invented by the person who invented Chocolateland?
   A yes
   B no
   C maybe

6 What information does the picture give that isn't made clear in the text?

   ....
   ....
   ....

Get creative

7 Make up the title for a game you'd like to eat.

Answers and explanations on page 115

68

Excel Advanced Skills: Year 1 Advanced English

UNIT 20A

READING AND COMPREHENSION

Bats

❶ Bats live in large groups and shelter together in caves and trees. You might have heard they sleep upside down. It's true: they hang from branches. They also sleep in the day and stay awake through the night. A famous poet* once wrote that bats have wings 'like bits of umbrella' and they hang themselves up 'like rows of disgusting old rags'.

❷ Bats are mammals—the only mammals who have wings and can fly. They live all over the world, including in Australia, but they like warmer places best. Some types mainly eat blossoms and fruit. Other types prefer insects and small animals such as frogs and mice.

❸ Bats are useful. They eat insects that harm plants and, like bees, they carry pollen to plants.

*DH Lawrence, 'Bat', 1923

1. Bats live
   - A alone.
   - B with their parents.
   - C in groups.

2. Bats sleep
   - A the right way up.
   - B upside down.
   - C curled into a ball.

3. Bats sleep
   - A in the night.
   - B in the day.
   - C through the day and the night.

4. Are there different types of bats?
   - A yes
   - B no
   - C maybe

5. What makes bats different from humans?
   - A They feed their young with milk.
   - B They live all over the world.
   - C They can fly.

6. Why might some people dislike bats? ....

☞ Answers and explanations on page 115

Excel Advanced Skills: Year 1 Advanced English

UNIT 20B

SPELLING

Write the correct spelling of the underlined words in questions 1–4.

1. I think bats' wings do look a bit like <u>umbreller</u> spokes!

   _____

2. Bats are <u>mamals</u>.

   _____

3. That bat likes eating <u>blossums</u>.

   _____

4. Some bats <u>manely</u> eat insects and small animals.

   _____

5. Change the first letter of **hang** to make three rhyming words.

   _____

   _____

VOCABULARY

6. Circle the word that has a similar meaning to the underlined word.

   Some insects <u>harm</u> plants.

   A swallow   B damage
   C hamper   D wound

7. Which word from the text means **choose above others**?

   _____

8. Add a word from the text to the sentence.

   Bats are the _____ mammals who can fly.

9. Circle the word that does **not** belong.

   A useful   B helpful
   C handy   D useless

GRAMMAR

10. Complete the sentence with a proper noun from the text.

    Bats live in many countries including _____.

11. Choose a verb or verb group from the box to correctly complete the sentence.

    | have | had | are having | have had |

    Bats _____ wings and can fly.

12. Write a word from the text to tell **how**.

    We saw bats sheltering _____ in a cave.

13. Choose a pronoun from the box to correctly complete the sentence.

    | he | she | it | you | they | I | we |

    I asked you when they slept but _____ didn't answer me.

PUNCTUATION

Rewrite the sentences correctly.

14. bats sleep upside down

    _____

    _____

15. some bats eat insects frogs and mice

    _____

    _____

TEXTS IN CONTEXT

UNIT 20C

Bats

❶ Bats live in large groups and shelter together in caves and trees. You might have heard they sleep upside down. It's true: they hang from branches. They also sleep in the day and stay awake through the night. A famous poet* once wrote that bats have wings 'like bits of umbrella' and they hang themselves up 'like rows of disgusting old rags'.

❷ Bats are mammals—the only mammals who have wings and can fly. They live all over the world, including in Australia, but they like warmer places best. Some types mainly eat blossoms and fruit. Other types prefer insects and small animals such as frogs and mice.

Bats are useful. They eat insects that harm plants and, like bees, they carry pollen to plants.

*DH Lawrence, 'Bat', 1923

1. The purpose of this text is to
   A inform.   B argue.   C persuade.

2. In which paragraph does the writer talk directly to the reader?
   A paragraph one   B paragraph two
   C paragraph three

3. Why does the writer talk directly to the reader?
   A to show off   B to shock
   C to get attention

4. The poet's words
   A explain how bats behave.
   B describe what bats look like to him.
   C give facts about bats.

5. The poet's words suggest
   A he admires bats.
   B he would like to own a bat.
   C he doesn't like the look of bats.

6. Do you think the writer of the text admires bats? Why or why not?

   ....

   ....

Get creative

7. Fill in the spaces with your own ideas.
   When spiders are asleep they look like ....
   When baby snakes are asleep they look like ....
   When wombats are asleep they look like ....

☞ Answers and explanations on page 116

Excel Advanced Skills: Year 1 Advanced English

READING AND COMPREHENSION

UNIT 21A

Making clay

Note: Have an adult nearby when you are using the stove.

Ingredients
- 1 cup baking soda
- ½ cup cornflour
- ¾ cup water
- Food colouring

Utensils
- Pot
- Bowl
- Wooden spoon or whisk
- Cover for bowl (e.g. wet tea towel)

What to do
- Mix everything together in a pot.
- Put the pot on a medium heat.
- Stir often until the mixture bubbles and then begins to clump together.
- Put mixture into bowl and cover.
- Leave until cool and dry.
- Knead the mixture together.
- Add food colouring and mix again.

Use your clay to make anything you like! What about an animal or maybe a planet such as Jupiter?

1. Under which heading is water?
   A Ingredients B Utensils C What to do

2. Under which heading is whisk?
   A Ingredients B Utensils C What to do

3. What kind of colouring do you add?
   A water B food C cornflour

4. What does the text **not** tell you?
   A which utensils you will need
   B what colour to make your clay
   C what you could cover the mixture with

5. Why do you need an adult nearby?
   A to make sure you are kept safe B to explain what to do C to have a friend with you

6. Name three things you could make with clay.

Answers and explanations on page 116

Excel Advanced Skills: Year 1 Advanced English

UNIT 21B

SPELLING

Write the correct spelling of the underlined words in questions 1–4.

1. Put your clay in the <u>bowel</u>, please.

   ....

2. Did you use a <u>woodden</u> spoon?

   ....

3. You must <u>need</u> the mixture with your hands.

   ....

4. Four <u>ingrediants</u> are needed to make clay.

   ....

5. Change the first letter of **heat** to make three rhyming words.

   ....

VOCABULARY

6. Circle the word that has a similar meaning to the underlined word.

   Did you <u>mix</u> the ingredients together?
   - A lump
   - B link
   - C blend
   - D fuse

7. Which word from the text means **a lump or mass**?

   ....

8. Add a word from the text to the sentence.

   You need to use a .... heat so it doesn't burn.

9. Circle the word that does **not** belong.
   - A everything
   - B something
   - C all
   - D nothing

GRAMMAR

10. Complete the sentence with a proper noun from the text.

    I used the clay I made to make the planet ....

11. Choose a verb or verb group from the box to correctly complete the sentence.

    | left | had left | leaves | leave |

    You should .... the mixture to cool.

12. Write a word from the text to tell **how**.

    Please stir the mixture .... while it is heating.

13. Choose a pronoun from the box to correctly complete the sentence.

    | he | she | it | you | they | I | we |

    You warm the mixture but then you let .... cool.

PUNCTUATION

Rewrite the sentences correctly.

14. she asked what I made with the clay

    ....
    ....

15. you will need a pot a bowl and a spoon

    ....
    ....

Answers and explanations on page 116

73

Excel Advanced Skills: Year 1 Advanced English

TEXTS IN CONTEXT

UNIT 21C

Making clay

Note: Have an adult nearby when you are using the stove.

Ingredients
- 1 cup baking soda
- ½ cup cornflour
- ¾ cup water
- Food colouring

Utensils
- Pot
- Bowl
- Wooden spoon or whisk
- Cover for bowl (e.g. wet tea towel)

What to do
- Mix everything together in a pot.
- Put the pot on a medium heat.
- Stir often until the mixture bubbles and then begins to clump together.
- Put mixture into bowl and cover.
- Leave until cool and dry.
- Knead the mixture together.
- Add food colouring and mix again.

Use your clay to make anything you like! What about an animal or maybe a planet such as Jupiter?

---

1. This text is a
   A speech.
   B recipe.
   C story.

2. It is written mainly for
   A children.
   B adults.
   C adults and children.

3. Why are the ingredients and utensils listed first?
   A so you can start making clay at once
   B so you can get ready to make clay
   C so you can look back at them once you begin making clay

4. Could the order of the items under **What to do** be changed?
   A yes   B no   C maybe

5. The first word of each dot point under **What to do** is
   A a rule.
   B a suggestion.
   C an instruction.

6. How is the picture connected to the text? Explain.

Get creative

7. Using the same headings as the text, write down how to make a drink of orange juice using real oranges.

Answers and explanations on page 116

READING AND COMPREHENSION

UNIT 22A

Tongue twisters

1. Try saying this sentence a few times very quickly: Fred fed Ted bread and Ted fed Fred bread. Did you get your words in a muddle? Most people do. It's because some sounds are very hard to say together quickly. That's the fun of tongue twisters.

2. One famous tongue twister, 'She sells seashells on the seashore', was made up more than 200 years ago. It was about a young girl called Mary. She used to dig up fossils and shells from a beach in England near where she lived. Then she'd sell them to make money for her family.

3. Mary would be shocked to learn she is still being talked about today!

---

1. What is fed to Ted and Fred?
   - **A** cheddar cheese
   - **B** morning tea
   - **C** bread

2. Where did Mary sell her shells?
   - **A** 200 years ago
   - **B** on the seashore
   - **C** for her family

3. How long ago was Mary selling shells?
   - **A** less than 200 years
   - **B** more than 200 years
   - **C** exactly 200 years

4. Which sounds are hard to say together quickly in the tongue twister about Mary?
   - **A** 's' and 'sh'
   - **B** 'sh' and 'll'
   - **C** 'th' and 'ea'

5. Do you think tongue twisters are fun? Why or why not?

   ....

   ....

6. Do you think Mary would be 'shocked' (line 12)? Why or why not?

   ....

   ....

☞ Answers and explanations on page 116

UNIT 22B

SPELLING

Write the correct spelling of the underlined words in questions 1–4.

1. That <u>sentance</u> is hard to say quickly.

   ....

2. I felt as if my tongue was in a <u>not</u>!

   ....

3. I'm really good at <u>tonge</u> twisters.

   ....

4. How <u>yung</u> was Mary when she sold shells?

   ....

5. Change the first letter of **near** to make three rhyming words.

   ....

VOCABULARY

6. Circle the words that have a similar meaning to the underlined word.

   She found them <u>near</u> where she lived.

   A on top of B across from
   C close by   D on the right of

7. Which word from the text means **remains of living things that lived long ago**?

   ....

8. Add a word from the text to the sentence.

   Can you work out which .... are hard to say together quickly?

9. Circle the word that does **not** belong.
   A muddle
   B mix-up
   C order
   D jumble

GRAMMAR

10. Complete the sentence with a proper noun from the text.

    Did Ted feed .... ?

11. Choose a verb from the box to correctly complete the sentence.

    | say | says | saying | said |

    Try .... this tongue twister right now.

12. Write a word from the text to tell **how**.

    You have to repeat the sentences ....

13. Choose a pronoun from the box to correctly complete the sentence.

    | he | she | it | you | they | I | we |

    Did Fred have the bread or did .... give it to Ted?

PUNCTUATION

Rewrite the sentences correctly.

14. he said fred fed ted bread

    ....
    ....

15. thats a shock

    ....
    ....

TEXTS IN CONTEXT

UNIT 22C

Tongue twisters

1. Try saying this sentence a few times very quickly: Fred fed Ted bread and Ted fed Fred bread. Did you get your words in a muddle? Most people do. It's because some sounds are very hard to say together quickly. That's the fun of tongue twisters.

2. One famous tongue twister, 'She sells seashells on the seashore', was made up more than 200 years ago. It was about a young girl called Mary. She used to dig up fossils and shells from a beach in England near where she lived. Then she'd sell them to make money for her family.

3. Mary would be shocked to learn she is still being talked about today!

---

1. This text aims to
   A tell a story about a girl.
   B share interesting information about tongue twisters.
   C describe how tongue twisters first began.

2. The writer wants readers to
   A enjoy playing with words and sounds.
   B learn good pronunciation.
   C learn which sounds must not be said.

3. Where could the definition of a tongue twister be added?
   A at the beginning of paragraph one.
   B at the end of paragraph two
   C at the beginning of paragraph three

4. Which sound is repeated three times in the title?
   A 't'   B 'u'   C 'i'

5. Which would make the best caption for the picture?
   A I've got a headache.
   B I think I've caught the flu.
   C Too many tongue twisters for me!

6. Which sentence is most difficult to say many times quickly?
   A Mary lived in England.
   B She sees cheese.
   C Tongue twisters are fun.

Get creative

7. Make up a short tongue twister of your own. Ask a friend to test it for you.

Answers and explanations on page 117

Excel Advanced Skills: Year 1 Advanced English

READING AND COMPREHENSION

UNIT 23A

1 **How is honey made?**

2 Who can we thank for the honey we find in
3 jars at the shops? We can thank the bees!

4 It all begins when bees leave their hives to
5 gather nectar. The bees suck nectar from
6 the flowers with their long tongues, then
7 they swallow it. It is stored in a honey sack
8 above their stomachs.

9 When the bees' honey sacks are full, they fly back to their hives. They
10 carefully pass the nectar to other bees. They store the chewed nectar in
11 wax-like tubes. The bees fan them to get the water out, then seal them
12 with something that hardens into beeswax. These are the honeycombs
13 that become our honey.

1. What do bees use to suck nectar from flowers?
   - **A** a honey sack
   - **B** their long tongues
   - **C** their wings

2. When do the bees fly back to their hives?
   - **A** when they are hungry
   - **B** when they feel sleepy
   - **C** when they have filled their honey sacks

3. How do the bees dry the chewed nectar?
   - **A** They use fans.
   - **B** They use their wings as fans.
   - **C** They turn on the heater.

4. Why do bees make honeycombs?
   - **A** to store food for themselves
   - **B** to make honey for humans
   - **C** to fill in the time

5. Bees can be described as
   - **A** lazy.
   - **B** hardworking.
   - **C** foolish.

6. How does the honey get from the hive into the jars?

   ....

   ....

Answers and explanations on page 117

UNIT 23B

SPELLING

Write the correct spelling of the underlined words in questions 1–4.

1. Pooh Bear liked to eat <u>honney</u>.

2. The bees have a sack above their <u>stumacks</u>.

3. The nectar is <u>chude</u> by the bees.

4. You can see the <u>honeycolm</u> in the picture.

5. Write three words from the word family that includes **begin**.

VOCABULARY

6. Circle the word that has a similar meaning to the underlined word.

   Bees <u>gather</u> nectar from flowers.
   - A pick
   - B steal
   - C collect
   - D poke

7. Which word from the text means **close off**?

8. Add a word from the text to the sentence.

   Bees use their _____ to get nectar from flowers.

9. Circle the word that does **not** belong.
   - A store
   - B keep
   - C waste
   - D hoard

GRAMMAR

10. Complete the sentence with a noun group from the text.

    The bees suck nectar from _____.

11. Choose a verb from the box to correctly complete the sentence.

    | found | finds | find | finding |

    Did you _____ a jar of honey at the shop?

12. Write a word from the text to tell **how**.

    Bees do their work _____.

13. Choose a word from the box to correctly complete the sentence.

    | and | so | but | because | or |

    The honey is put in jars _____ people can buy it in the shops.

PUNCTUATION

Rewrite the sentences correctly.

14. what beautiful honey

15. where do bees store nectar

UNIT 23C

TEXTS IN CONTEXT

1 **How is honey made?**

2 Who can we thank for the honey we find in
3 jars at the shops? We can thank the bees!

4 It all begins when bees leave their hives to
5 gather nectar. The bees suck nectar from
6 the flowers with their long tongues, then
7 they swallow it. It is stored in a honey sack
8 above their stomachs.

9 When the bees' honey sacks are full, they fly back to their hives. They
10 carefully pass the nectar to other bees. They store the chewed nectar in
11 wax-like tubes. The bees fan them to get the water out, then seal them
12 with something that hardens into beeswax. These are the honeycombs
13 that become our honey.

1. This text
   A tells a story.
   B tells how something is done.
   C sells a product.

2. Where would you read a text like this?
   A in a recipe book
   B in a storybook
   C in a book about insects

3. The text begins with a question to
   A catch the reader's interest.
   B make the reader feel worried.
   C trick the reader.

4. The text includes words that are
   A poetic.
   B scientific.
   C musical.

5. The writer _____ bees.
   A admires
   B is afraid of
   C dislikes

6. Would this picture have been a better choice for the text? Why or why not?

   ....

   ....

Get creative

7. Find out the answers to these questions.
   How many legs does a honey bee have?
   How many body parts does it have?
   How many wings does it have?

Answers and explanations on page 117

NAPLAN-style Reading Test 3

King Midas

King Midas was a very rich king. Even so, all he could think of was getting more and more gold. He was sure it was being rich that made him happy.

One day, one of the gods gave King Midas a wish. It was to reward him for a kind deed to one of the god's friends. King Midas wished for everything he touched to turn to gold. Next morning that is exactly what happened. Clothes, food, everything. Even his daughter when he hugged her!

The god felt sorry for King Midas and told him to wash his hands in the river. The gold flowed away. King Midas was very grateful and from then on he was a wiser and less greedy king.

1. How many wishes was King Midas given?
   A one
   B two
   C three

2. Who lived in the palace with King Midas?
   A his friend
   B a god
   C his daughter

3. The daughter of King Midas
   A disappeared.
   B became a golden statue.
   C became a gold coin.

4. The wish King Midas made was a _____ choice.
   A foolish
   B wise
   C good

5. How would King Midas have felt when his wish came true?
   A pleased
   B horrified
   C worried

6. Was King Midas an evil person?
   A No, he could also be kind.
   B Yes, he was cruel and nasty.
   C Yes, he turned his daughter into a statue.

7. What lesson does this story teach?
   A Better late than never.
   B Greed is its own reward.
   C Be careful what you wish for.

Answers and explanations on page 117

NAPLAN-style Conventions of Language Test 3

The spelling mistakes in these sentences have been underlined. Write the correct spelling on the lines.

1. My <u>fahther</u> likes to read books.

   ....

2. The <u>chilldren</u> are at school this morning.

   ....

3. Ben <u>frew</u> the ball into the net.

   ....

4. <u>Were</u> is everyone hiding?

   ....

5. Mum doesn't have <u>shugar</u> in her tea anymore.

   ....

Read the text. Choose the correct word to complete the sentences.

> Mary had a little lamb. It ......(6)...... her to school one day. Mary had to ......(7)...... her lamb home. When she got home she put the lamb in the field and shut the gate ......(8)...... her.

6. A followed   B follows
   C will follow

7. A took   B take
   C taken

8. A with   B over
   C behind

9. Underline the proper noun in this sentence.

   I am going to play football with Sally tomorrow.

10. Complete the sentence with the correct verb or verb group.

    I .... a race at our swimming carnival this morning.
    A win
    B winned
    C won
    D were winning

11. Underline the word that tells **how**.

    He ate greedily until he was more than full!

12. Which pronoun correctly completes the sentence?

    Mum and I went shopping and .... bought a present for each other.
    A she
    B I
    C we
    D they

13. Which sentence is punctuated correctly?
    A Have you lived in australia for long.
    B Have you lived in australia for long?
    C Have you lived in Australia for long?
    D Have you lived in Australia for long!

14. Which sentence is **not** punctuated correctly?
    A He said he'd lend me his book.
    B Thats a really good idea.
    C Will you be ready in time?
    D I've had some very exciting news!

Answers and explanations on page 117

82   *Excel* Advanced Skills: **Year 1 Advanced English**

READING AND COMPREHENSION

UNIT 24A

1 ***Josephine Wants To Dance* by Jackie French**

2 *Josephine Wants To Dance* is written by Jackie French. It is a favourite book
3 of mine. Josephine is a kangaroo who lives in the bush. She grows up
4 wanting to be a dancer! She never gives up her dream even when other
5 people tell her she's silly. At first it makes you
6 laugh to see a kangaroo dancing but soon she is
7 a really good dancer. Then there is a wonderful
8 surprise for Josephine near the end. I won't spoil
9 it for you.

10 The book has been made into a musical. We are
11 going to see it on my birthday and I can't wait.

12 by Maximo

---

1. Who wrote *Josephine Wants to Dance*?
   - A Josephine
   - B Maximo
   - C Jackie French

2. When will Maximo see the musical?
   - A next week
   - B on his birthday
   - C when he grows up

3. When does Josephine get a surprise?
   - A near the end of the story
   - B on her birthday
   - C when she gives up her dream

4. Some people think Josephine is silly because
   - A kangaroos cannot be dancers.
   - B kangaroos should not be dreamers.
   - C Josephine makes you laugh.

5. 'I won't spoil it for you' (lines 8–9) means
   - A I'll tell you about the surprise later.
   - B I know you've guessed it will be a musical.
   - C I won't tell you about the surprise.

6. What makes Josephine a good dancer?

   _____

   _____

Answers and explanations on page 117

83

Excel Advanced Skills: Year 1 Advanced English

UNIT 24B

SPELLING

Write the correct spelling of the underlined words in questions 1–4.

1. Josephine wants to be a <u>danser</u>.

   ....

2. She has a <u>dreem</u>.

   ....

3. It's a <u>favorit</u> book of mine.

   ....

4. She made me <u>larf</u> at first.

   ....

5. Write three words from the word family that includes **dance**.

   ....

   ....

VOCABULARY

6. Circle the word that has a similar meaning to the underlined word.

   That's not one of my <u>favourite</u> books.
   - A best-loved
   - B main
   - C popular
   - D pet

7. Which word from the text means **a play or film with lots of singing and dancing**?

   ....

8. Add a word from the text to the sentence.

   The surprise comes near the .... of the story.

9. Circle the word that does **not** belong.
   - A repair
   - B spoil
   - C build
   - D fix

GRAMMAR

10. Complete the sentence with a noun group from the text.

    Josephine is ....

    ....

11. Choose a verb or verb group from the box to correctly complete the sentence.

    | see | sees | saw | has seen |

    We are going to .... the musical soon.

12. Write words from the text to tell **where**.

    Josephine lives ....

    ....

13. Choose a word from the box to correctly complete the sentence.

    | and | so | but | because | or |

    Josephine has a dream .... she never gives up.

PUNCTUATION

Rewrite the sentences correctly.

14. do you have a favourite book

    ....

    ....

15. ive never seen a dancing kangaroo

    ....

    ....

TEXTS IN CONTEXT

UNIT 24C

1 **Josephine Wants To Dance by Jackie French**

2 *Josephine Wants To Dance* is written by Jackie French. It is a favourite book
3 of mine. Josephine is a kangaroo who lives in the bush. She grows up
4 wanting to be a dancer! She never gives up her dream even when other
5 people tell her she's silly. At first it makes you
6 laugh to see a kangaroo dancing but soon she is
7 a really good dancer. Then there is a wonderful
8 surprise for Josephine near the end. I won't spoil
9 it for you.

10 The book has been made into a musical. We are
11 going to see it on my birthday and I can't wait.

12 by Maximo

1 The text is
   A an advertisement.
   B a review.
   C a recount.

2 Maximo mainly wants to
   A encourage others to read the book.
   B explain what the surprise is in the book.
   C tell others about his birthday.

3 Put the information in the order in which it appears in the text.

   A what the book is about

   B the name of the book

   C why it is a favourite book

4 Maximo admires Josephine because she
   A doesn't give up.
   B makes him laugh.
   C is in a musical.

5 'She never gives up her dream' (line 4). What is her dream?

   ....
   ....

6 Do you think the book will have a happy ending? Why or why not?

   ....
   ....
   ....
   ....

Get creative

7 Write the name and author of a book you think others would enjoy reading.
   Then write a sentence that gives a reason for your choice.

Answers and explanations on page 118

85

Excel Advanced Skills: Year 1 Advanced English

READING AND COMPREHENSION

UNIT 25A

Moreton Bay Figs

Moreton Bay Figs are very big trees. They are famous for their size. Their trunks can grow to two and a half metres around. That's roughly two huge steps and a normal-size one. They can grow very, very tall—at times up to 50 metres. That's about half the length of a soccer field or eight times as tall as a giraffe! Their big roots can grow to nine metres above the soil and spread for about 30 metres.

Birds, bats and possums like to feast on the purple fruit of Moreton Bay Figs. Children like to climb all over them.

1. What are Moreton Bay Figs famous for?
   - A their trunks
   - B their name
   - C their size

2. Moreton Bay Figs grow
   - A quite tall.
   - B very tall.
   - C fairly tall.

3. What grows eight times as tall as a giraffe?
   - A a soccer field
   - B the roots of a Moreton Bay Fig
   - C a Moreton Bay Fig

4. Could you wrap your arms around a full-size Moreton Bay Fig?
   - A yes
   - B no
   - C maybe

5. The roots can grow
   - A taller than the trunk of the tree.
   - B to the height of nine huge steps.
   - C as tall as a soccer field.

6. Are Moreton Bay Figs useful trees? Why or why not?

....

....

☞ Answers and explanations on page 118

UNIT 25B

SPELLING

Write the correct spelling of the underlined words in questions 1–4.

1. They are famous for their <u>sise</u>.

   ....

2. Fifty metres is <u>harf</u> the length of a soccer field.

   ....

3. <u>Posums</u> like to feast on figs.

   ....

4. Figs are a type of <u>froot</u>.

   ....

5. Write three words from the word family that includes **grow**.

   ....

   ....

VOCABULARY

6. Circle the word that has a similar meaning to the underlined word.

   Can you take two <u>huge</u> steps?
   - A big
   - B enormous
   - C normal
   - D medium

7. Which word from the text means **well-known by many**?

   ....

   ....

8. Add a word from the text to the sentence.

   The roots can .... for about 30 metres.

9. Circle the word that does **not** belong.
   - A roughly
   - B about
   - C exactly
   - D around

GRAMMAR

10. Complete the sentence with a noun group from the text.

    The tree's roots grow above ....
    ....

11. Choose a verb from the box to correctly complete the sentence.

    | climb | climbs | climbed | climbing |

    Have you ever .... a Moreton Bay Fig?

12. Write words from the text to tell **when**.

    .... ,
    Moreton Bay Fig trees reach 50 metres.

13. Choose a word from the box to correctly complete the sentence.

    | and | so | but | because | or |

    The tree is fun to climb .... it has such big branches.

PUNCTUATION

Rewrite the sentences correctly.

14. do possums eat the figs

    ....

    ....

15. theres a moreton bay fig tree in our park

    ....

    ....

    ....

Answers and explanations on page 118

87

Excel Advanced Skills: Year 1 Advanced English

TEXTS IN CONTEXT

UNIT 25C

Moreton Bay Figs

Moreton Bay Figs are very big trees. They are famous for their size. Their trunks can grow to two and a half metres around. That's roughly two huge steps and a normal-size one. They can grow very, very tall—at times up to 50 metres. That's about half the length of a soccer field or eight times as tall as a giraffe! Their big roots can grow to nine metres above the soil and spread for about 30 metres.

Birds, bats and possums like to feast on the purple fruit of Moreton Bay Figs. Children like to climb all over them.

1. The purpose of this text is to
   A give information.
   B tell how to do something.
   C persuade people to act.

2. You could find this text in
   A a newspaper.
   B an advertisement.
   C Wikipedia (an online encyclopedia).

3. The first paragraph is mainly about the Moreton Bay Fig tree's
   A colour.
   B size.
   C shape.

4. The writer compares the size of parts of the tree to other things
   A to help the reader imagine their size more clearly.
   B to show how beautiful the tree is.
   C to show why people don't have these trees in their gardens.

5. The exclamation mark (line 6) suggests the author is
   A worried.
   B amused.
   C impressed.

6. The people in the picture help you understand
   A what type of fruit is on the tree.
   B the size of the tree.
   C what type of tree it is.

Get creative

7. Find out how Indigenous Australians used Moreton Bay Fig trees.

Answers and explanations on page 118

88

Excel Advanced Skills: Year 1 Advanced English

READING AND COMPREHENSION

UNIT 26A

From 'The Duck and the Kangaroo' by Edward Lear

Said the Duck to the Kangaroo,
'Good gracious! how you hop
Over the fields, and the water too,
As if you never would stop!
My life is a bore in this nasty pond;
And I long to go out in the world
   beyond:
I wish I could hop like you,'
Said the Duck to the Kangaroo.

…

Said the Kangaroo, 'I'm ready,
All in the moonlight pale;
But to balance me well, dear
   Duck, sit steady,
And quite at the end of my tail.'

So away they went with a hop
   and a bound;
And they hopped the whole
   world three times round.
And who so happy, oh! who,
As the Duck and the Kangaroo?

1. Who speaks first?
   A The Duck   B The Kangaroo   C The Duck and the Kangaroo

2. Where does the Duck live?
   A in the fields   B near the water   C in a pond

3. How many times do the Duck and the Kangaroo circle the world?
   A once   B twice   C three times

4. Why is the Duck unhappy?
   A It doesn't have any friends.   B It finds life boring.   C People are nasty to it.

5. How does the Duck feel about the Kangaroo's way of life?
   A puzzled   B envious   C worried

6. How does the Kangaroo solve the Duck's problems?

   ....

   ....

Answers and explanations on page 118

UNIT 26B

SPELLING

Write the correct spelling of the underlined words in questions 1–4.

1. The kangaroo hoped across the fields.

   ....

2. Everything looked pale in the moonlite.

   ....

3. I am not qwite ready yet.

   ....

4. Please sit on the end of my tale.

   ....

5. Write three words from the word family that includes **sale**.

   ....

VOCABULARY

6. Circle the word that has a similar meaning to the underlined word.

   I don't like living in this nasty place!
   - A ugly
   - B horrid
   - C evil
   - D different

7. Add a word from the text to the sentence.

   They've been around the .... world more than once!

8. Which word from the text means **put something in a steady position so it doesn't fall**?

   ....

9. Circle the word that does **not** belong.
   - A fear
   - B hope
   - C wish
   - D dream

GRAMMAR

10. Complete the sentence with a noun group from the text.

    The Duck spoke to ....

11. Choose a verb from the box to correctly complete the sentence.

    | say | says | saying | said |

    The Kangaroo .... he was ready to take off now.

12. Write words from the text to tell **where**.

    You need to sit ...., dear Duck, or I won't be able to hop.

13. Choose a word from the box to correctly complete the sentence.

    | and | so | but | because | or |

    Would you rather be a duck .... a kangaroo?

PUNCTUATION

Rewrite the sentences correctly.

14. will you take me with you I asked

    ....

    ....

15. i wish I could hop like you he said

    ....

    ....

☞ Answers and explanations on pages 118–119

90

Excel Advanced Skills: Year 1 Advanced English

TEXTS IN CONTEXT

UNIT 26C

From 'The Duck and the Kangaroo' by Edward Lear

Said the Duck to the Kangaroo,
'Good gracious! how you hop
Over the fields, and the water too,
As if you never would stop!
My life is a bore in this nasty pond;
And I long to go out in the world
    beyond:
I wish I could hop like you,'
Said the Duck to the Kangaroo.

…

Said the Kangaroo, 'I'm ready,
All in the moonlight pale;
But to balance me well, dear Duck,
    sit steady,
And quite at the end of my tail.'

So away they went with a hop and
    a bound;
And they hopped the whole
    world three times round.
And who so happy, oh! who,
As the Duck and the Kangaroo?

The Duck and the Kangaroo

---

1. What is the purpose of the poem?
   A to entertain
   B to describe how animals behave
   C to report something important

2. You would find this poem in a book
   A about animal habits.
   B of nonsense verse.
   C about real adventures.

3. In what order do these events happen?
   A The Duck balances on the Kangaroo's tail. ☐
   B The Duck watches the Kangaroo hopping. ☐
   C They travel around the world together. ☐

4. Why does the poet put the word **pale** after **moonlight**?
   A to set up the rhyme with tail
   B to show how beautiful it is
   C to show it is not daytime

5. This poem does **not** have
   A a strong rhythm.
   B the same rhyming pattern in each stanza.
   C a serious meaning.

6. Are the two characters similar or different? Explain.

   ....
   ....

Get creative

7. Read the missing part of Edward Lear's poem 'The Duck and the Kangaroo'. You will find it in the library or online. How many stars out of five would you give it? (Five is excellent and one is not very good.) Explain your choice.

☞ Answers and explanations on page 119

91

Excel Advanced Skills: Year 1 Advanced English

READING AND COMPREHENSION

UNIT 27A

1 **When Tim met Peter Rabbit**

2 Once upon a time Tim was playing in his garden. He saw a flash of
3 colour. He looked again and saw two ears and a powder-puff tail.
4 Could it be?

5 "Good morning," the rabbit said.

6 "Good morning, Peter Rabbit," Tim replied boldly.

7 "Would you mind if I had a few carrots for my
8 family?" the rabbit asked.

9 "Have as many as you need," Tim replied.

10 Tim never forgot that meeting. For the rest of his life, he believed
11 animals from storybooks could really come to life!

1 What was Tim doing when he saw the rabbit?
   - A digging up carrots
   - B searching for rabbits
   - C playing in his garden

2 What did Tim never forget?
   - A his meeting with Peter Rabbit
   - B his storybooks
   - C the flash of blue

3 What did the rabbit want?
   - A a friendly chat
   - B to meet Tim
   - C carrots for the family

4 Tim thought the flash of colour was Peter Rabbit's
   - A jacket.
   - B hat.
   - C trousers.

5 Where had Tim learnt about Peter Rabbit?
   - A from his parents
   - B from a storybook
   - C from a farmer

6 Do you think Tim saw Peter Rabbit in his garden? Explain.

....

....

....

Answers and explanations on page 119

UNIT 27B

SPELLING

Write the correct spelling of the underlined words in questions 1–4.

1. What colour is the rabbit's <u>tale</u>?

   ....

2. You should eat your <u>carots</u>.

   ....

3. He <u>beleived</u> the rabbit was Peter.

   ....

4. The rabbit <u>repleid</u> to Tim.

   ....

5. Write three words from the word family that includes **play**.

   ....
   ....

VOCABULARY

6. Circle the word that has a similar meaning to the underlined word.

   Tim spoke and the rabbit <u>replied</u>.
   - A answered
   - B spoke
   - C returned
   - D asked

7. Which word from the text means **thought it was true**?

   ....

8. Add a word from the text to the sentence.

   Tim never .... his meeting with Peter Rabbit.

9. Circle the word that does **not** belong.
   - A flash
   - B glimmer
   - C stream
   - D gleam

GRAMMAR

10. Complete the sentence with a noun group from the text.

    "Good morning," said ....
    ....

11. Choose a verb from the box to correctly complete the sentence.

    | come | comes | came | coming |

    Can storybook animals .... to life?

12. Write words from the text to tell **where**.

    The rabbit visited Tim ....
    ....

13. Choose a word from the box to correctly complete the sentence.

    | and | so | but | because | or |

    The rabbit was either Peter .... it wasn't him at all.

PUNCTUATION

Rewrite the sentences correctly.

14. ive read a story about peter rabbit

    ....
    ....
    ....

15. have as many as you want said tim

    ....
    ....
    ....

Answers and explanations on page 119

93

Excel Advanced Skills: Year 1 Advanced English

UNIT 27C

TEXTS IN CONTEXT

1 **When Tim met Peter Rabbit**

2 Once upon a time Tim was playing in his garden. He saw a flash of
3 colour. He looked again and saw two ears and a powder-puff tail.
4 Could it be?

5 "Good morning," the rabbit said.

6 "Good morning, Peter Rabbit," Tim replied boldly.

7 "Would you mind if I had a few carrots for my
8 family?" the rabbit asked.

9 "Have as many as you need," Tim replied.

10 Tim never forgot that meeting. For the rest of his life, he believed
11 animals from storybooks could really come to life!

---

1. This text
   A gives an explanation.
   B tells a story.
   C describes something.

2. Who tells what happens in the text?
   A Tim
   B Peter
   C the author

3. When does the action happen?
   A not long ago
   B a time in the past
   C in the garden

4. The rabbit's tail is compared to a powder puff because it
   A feels soft and fluffy.
   B smells like powder.
   C is easy to see.

5. What is bold about Tim's greeting (line 6)?
   A He dares to give the rabbit a name.
   B He is being cheeky and rude.
   C He feels shy speaking to a rabbit.

6. Did you like the text? Why or why not?

   ....
   ....
   ....
   ....

Get creative

7. Which storybook animal or person would you like to talk to?

Answers and explanations on page 119

94

Excel Advanced Skills: Year 1 Advanced English

READING AND COMPREHENSION

UNIT 28A

Chinese Dragons

❶ Dragons stand for power, strength and good luck in China.

❷ Dragons are part of Chinese New Year celebrations. People use poles to hold up the head and body of a dragon costume as they dance through the streets. Dragon dances are said to scare away bad spirits and bring good luck to everyone.

❸ Dragon-boat racing has been part of festivals in China for over 2000 years. A dragon's head (made up of part ox, part deer and part horse) is placed on the prow. The paddles make the dragon's claws. The scales of a snake are carved onto the body of the boat. Its tail is put on the stern. Dragon-boat races are now held all over the world.

1. What do people use to hold up their dragon costume?
   - A paddles
   - B poles
   - C scales

2. Dragon-boat races are now held
   - A only in China.
   - B everywhere except China.
   - C all over the world.

3. What are dragon dances said to scare away?
   - A bad spirits
   - B good luck
   - C snakes

4. Which part of the deer is used in the dragon's head?
   - A its antlers
   - B its scales
   - C its hooves

5. Which statement is **not** true?
   - A At Chinese New Year, real dragons dance in the streets.
   - B Dragon-boat races are popular.
   - C Dragons play an important part in Chinese people's beliefs.

6. What do Chinese people think of dragons? _____

☞ Answers and explanations on page 119

Excel Advanced Skills: Year 1 Advanced English

UNIT 28B

SPELLING

Write the correct spelling of the underlined words in questions 1–4.

1. Have you ever seen a <u>draggon</u>?

   ....

2. It is <u>Chineese</u> New Year next week.

   ....

3. Its <u>scailes</u> are like those of a snake.

   ....

4. <u>It's</u> tail is at the back of the boat.

   ....

5. Write three words from the word family that includes **race**.

   ....

   ....

VOCABULARY

6. Circle the word that has a similar meaning to the underlined word.

   They say dragons have <u>power</u> over rain, water and storms.

   A strength   B gifts
   C control   D light

7. Which word from the text means **piece of the whole**?

   ....

8. Add a word from the text to the sentence.

   You are likely to see a dragon at

   .... New Year.

9. Circle the word that does **not** belong.

   A frighten
   B scare
   C alarm
   D calm

GRAMMAR

10. Complete the sentence with a noun group from the text.

    ....

    are used as the dragon's claws.

11. Choose a verb from the box to correctly complete the sentence.

    | were | is | are | being |

    Chinese New Year .... a time of celebration.

12. Write words from the text to tell **where**. Dragon-boat racing has taken place

    ....

    ....

    for over 2000 years.

13. Choose a word from the box to correctly complete the sentence.

    | and | so | but | because | or |

    Dragon-boat racing .... dragon dances are both popular in China.

PUNCTUATION

Rewrite the sentences correctly.

14. chinese new year is held early in the year

    ....

    ....

15. the dragon parade was very exciting

    ....

    ....

☞ Answers and explanations on pages 119–120

TEXTS IN CONTEXT

UNIT **28C**

Chinese Dragons

❶ Dragons stand for power, strength and good luck in China.

❷ Dragons are part of Chinese New Year celebrations. People use poles to hold up the head and body of a dragon costume as they dance through the streets. Dragon dances are said to scare away bad spirits and bring good luck to everyone.

❸ Dragon-boat racing has been part of festivals in China for over 2000 years. A dragon's head (made up of part ox, part deer and part horse) is placed on the prow. The paddles make the dragon's claws. The scales of a snake are carved onto the body of the boat. Its tail is put on the stern. Dragon-boat races are now held all over the world.

1 This text is about
   A what dragons do.
   B what part dragons play in Chinese life.
   C why dragons are put on boats.

2 The purpose of the text is to
   A give factual information.
   B tell a story.
   C retell events.

3 'Each team in a race has a drummer on board.' Where could you add this sentence?
   A after the first sentence of paragraph one
   B at the beginning of paragraph two
   C before the last sentence of paragraph three

4 Who would always use the words prow and stern instead of front and back?
   A doctors
   B sailors
   C vets

5 To which sport is dragon-boat racing similar?
   A waterskiing
   B windsurfing
   C rowing

6 Would you like to take part in a dragon-boat race? Why or why not?

   ....
   ....

Get creative

7 Look at pictures of dragons on the internet then draw and colour your own dragon. Write a sentence about your dragon.

☞ Answers and explanations on page 120

Excel Advanced Skills: Year 1 Advanced English

READING AND COMPREHENSION

UNIT 29A

Trim

Trim was born at sea in 1797 on a ship on its way to Australia. He was chosen from a litter of cats by the ship's captain, Matthew Flinders. Trim was jet black all over except for a white star on his chest and white feet. Flinders wrote that Trim's feet looked as if they 'had been dipped in snow'. Sometimes Trim fell overboard! But he could swim and when a rope was thrown to him he ran up it like greased lightning to safety.

Trim sailed with Flinders around the world. Later he sailed with him around Australia—this was the first time this had been done! Today there are statues of Trim in several cities.

1. Where was Trim born?
   - A in the sea
   - B on a ship
   - C in 1797

2. Could Trim swim?
   - A yes
   - B no
   - C maybe

3. What shape was the white fur on trim's chest?
   - A oval-shaped
   - B moon-shaped
   - C star-shaped

4. Why did the sailors throw Trim a rope?
   - A so he could play games
   - B so he could sharpen his claws
   - C so he could get out of the water

5. What made Matthew Flinders famous?
   - A He sailed with a famous cat.
   - B He sailed around the world and around Australia.
   - C He was a ship's captain

6. Was Trim an unusual cat? Why or why not? _____

Answers and explanations on page 120

UNIT 29B

SPELLING

Write the correct spelling of the underlined words in questions 1–4.

1. Trim was part of a <u>liter</u>.

2. He has <u>wite</u> feet.

3. Which kitten would you have <u>chozen</u>?

4. Trim fell <u>overbored</u>!

5. Write three words from the word family that includes **wrote**.

VOCABULARY

6. Circle the word that has a similar meaning to the underlined word.

    His feet looked as if they'd been <u>dipped</u> in snow.
    - A dunked
    - B soaked
    - C washed
    - D drowned

7. Which word from the text means **more than two but not many**?

8. Add a word from the text to the sentence.

    He was chosen from a _____ of six kittens.

9. Circle the word that does **not** belong.
    - A only
    - B single
    - C first
    - D one

GRAMMAR

10. Complete the sentence with a noun group from the text.

    Trim was born on _____.

11. Choose a verb or verb group from the box to correctly complete the sentence.

    | fall | falls | fell | is falling |

    Trim _____ overboard twice yesterday!

12. Write words from the text to tell **how**.

    Trim could run up a rope _____.

13. Choose a word from the box to correctly complete the sentence.

    | and | so | but | because | or |

    I would love to see Trim's statue _____ I haven't been able to find one.

PUNCTUATION

Rewrite the sentences correctly.

14. cat overboard

15. the captain named his cat trim

TEXTS IN CONTEXT

UNIT 29C

Trim

Trim was born at sea in 1797 on a ship on its way to Australia. He was chosen from a litter of cats by the ship's captain, Matthew Flinders. Trim was jet black all over except for a white star on his chest and white feet. Flinders wrote that Trim's feet looked as if they 'had been dipped in snow'. Sometimes Trim fell overboard! But he could swim and when a rope was thrown to him he ran up it like greased lightning to safety.

Trim sailed with Flinders around the world. Later he sailed with him around Australia—this was the first time this had been done! Today there are statues of Trim in several cities.

1 This text gives a short account of
   A the life of Matthew Flinders.
   B the life of Trim.
   C the history of Australia.

2 Where would you find this text?
   A on a noticeboard
   B in a book about how to care for your cat
   C in a book about famous animals

3 In which order is this information given?

   A what Trim looked like ☐

   B what Trim did during his life ☐

   C when and where Trim was born ☐

4 Trim's feet look as if dipped in snow (line 8) because
   A his feet were snowy white all over.
   B his feet went white with cold.
   C he often played in snow.

5 What do you learn about Trim in the text that is not in the picture?

....

....

6 Do you think Matthew Flinders was fond of Trim? Why or why not?

....

....

....

Get creative

7 Find out the names of these statues:
The tortoise who died in 2006, aged 175:

....

The longest living hearing guide dog who died in 1995, aged 20:

....

☞ Answers and explanations on page 120

READING AND COMPREHENSION

UNIT 30A

1. **Two poems**
2. **Text 1: Where is it?**
3. In the day, the moon's not always
4. there—it's nowhere in the sky.
5. But in the night, it's shiny bright.
6. Can someone tell me why?
(Donna Gibbs, 2018)

7. **Text 2: Who was it?**
8. Of course I've heard the moon's green cheese,
9. But will somebody tell me, please,
10. Who was it took so big a bite
11. There's scarcely any left to-night?
(Evaleen Stein, 1918)

1. How does the moon look at night in Text 1?
   - **A** You can't see it.
   - **B** like green cheese
   - **C** shiny bright

2. How does the moon look in the day in Text 1?
   - **A** You can't see it.
   - **B** like green cheese
   - **C** shiny bright

3. The writer of Text 2 thinks the moon she sees has
   - **A** turned into cheese.
   - **B** had a bite taken out of it.
   - **C** shrunk.

4. Is there an answer to the question asked in Text 1?
   - **A** yes
   - **B** no
   - **C** maybe

5. Is there an answer to the question asked in Text 2?
   - **A** yes
   - **B** no
   - **C** maybe

6. Are the titles similar?

Answers and explanations on page 120

Excel Advanced Skills: Year 1 Advanced English

UNIT 30B

SPELLING

Write the correct spelling of the underlined words in questions 1–4.

1. Tonight the moon is <u>shinny</u> bright.

   ....

2. Is <u>sumone</u> there?

   ....

3. Could you <u>pleese</u> answer me?

   ....

4. There was <u>scarsely</u> any left.

   ....

5. Write three words from the word family that includes **heard**.

   ....

   ....

VOCABULARY

6. Circle the word that has a similar meaning to the underlined word.

   There's <u>scarcely</u> any left tonight.
   - A hardly
   - B slightly
   - C almost
   - D lastly

7. Add a word from the text to the sentence.

   Nobody can tell me .... the moon is in the daytime!

8. Which word from the text means **in or at no place; not anywhere**?

   ....

9. Circle the word that does **not** belong.
   - A nowhere
   - B somewhere
   - C disappeared
   - D vanished

GRAMMAR

10. Complete the sentence with a noun group from the text.

    In ...., the moon's not always there.

11. Choose a verb from the box to correctly complete the sentence.

is	are	was	were

    Sometimes you .... only able to see the moon at night.

12. Write words from the text to tell **when**.

    The moon looks shiny bright ....

    ....

13. Choose a word from the box to correctly complete the sentence.

and	so	but	because	or

    The questions are similar .... they are not exactly the same.

PUNCTUATION

Rewrite the sentences correctly.

14. its quite a puzzle

    ....

    ....

15. everyone knows the moons made of cheese

    ....

    ....

    ....

Answers and explanations on page 121

UNIT 30C

TEXTS IN CONTEXT

1 **Two poems**

2 **Text 1 Where is it?**

3 In the day, the moon's not always
4 there—it's nowhere in the sky.
5 But in the night, it's shiny bright.
6 Can someone tell me why?
(Donna Gibbs, 2018)

7 **Text 2 Who was it?**

8 Of course I've heard the moon's green cheese,
9 But will somebody tell me, please,
10 Who was it took so big a bite
11 There's scarcely any left to-night?
(Evaleen Stein, 1918)

1. The texts are
   - **A** stories.
   - **B** poems.
   - **C** plays.

2. The purpose of Text 2 is to
   - **A** make you laugh.
   - **B** make you think.
   - **C** make you scared.

3. Does it matter in which order you read Text 1 and Text 2?
   - **A** yes
   - **B** no
   - **C** maybe

4. Text 1 and Text 2
   - **A** ask the same question.
   - **B** answer the questions they ask.
   - **C** leave their questions unanswered.

5. Does the picture suit both Text 1 and Text 2? Explain.

6. Which poem do you prefer? Why?

Get creative

7. Make up a four-line rhyming poem either:
   - about the moon, the stars or the night sky

     or

   - which asks a question.

Answers and explanations on page 121

103

Excel Advanced Skills: Year 1 Advanced English

NAPLAN-style Reading Test 4

One lucky possum

A young boy, Joel Smith, found a possum this morning. It was in a park near the boy's home. The possum had trapped its head inside an empty honey jar. The jar had fallen out of an overflowing rubbish bin. The poor possum couldn't get its head out of the jar!

Joel ran home and asked his mother to call for help. Soon an ambulance for animals arrived. The officer wrapped the possum's feet in some towels. Then he carefully eased the possum's head out of the jar. The lucky possum ate some apple and then ran off into the bush.

1. Where did Joel find the possum?
   A at Joel's house
   B in the bush
   C in a park

2. Why did the possum put its head in the jar?
   A to see if its head fitted
   B to play a game
   C to eat the honey

3. Where was the empty jar?
   A in the bin
   B on the ground
   C at Joel's house

4. What was the possum's problem?
   A Its head was stuck.
   B It couldn't reach the bottom of the jar.
   C The bin was full.

5. Why did the officer wrap the possum's feet in towels?
   A to keep them warm
   B to make it comfortable
   C to stop its claws scratching

6. Where would you read this story?
   A in a diary
   B on a noticeboard
   C in a newspaper

7. Why was the possum lucky?
   A It found some apple to eat.
   B It was rescued with Joel's help.
   C Its feet were wrapped in towels.

Answers and explanations on page 121

NAPLAN-style Conventions of Language Test 4

There is one spelling mistake in each sentence. Write the correct spelling on the line.

1. Can you sale in your boat?

   ....

2. I have onely one soccer ball.

   ....

3. Please come becuase you will have fun.

   ....

4. Wood you be able to help me, please?

   ....

5. He doesn't have manny toys.

   ....

Read the text. Choose the correct word to complete the sentences.

> The sun, moon and stars ......(6)...... in outer space. There is no air there. People can't ......(7)...... in space. The gaps ......(8)...... the stars and planets are filled with gas and dust.

6. **A** is   **B** was
   C are   **D** were

7. **A** breathe   **B** breath
   C breathing   **D** breathed

8. **A** over   **B** between
   C under   **D** inside

9. Which word is a noun in the sentence?
   I like to climb up high in this tall tree.
   A I   **B** climb
   C high   **D** tree

10. Complete the sentence with the correct verb or verb group.
    We _____ into the city on a train yesterday.
    A go   **B** are going
    C went   **D** gone

11. Which words tell **where**?
    Nick was cross because his friend hit the ball out of the court.
    A Nick was cross
    B because his friend
    C hit the ball
    D out of the court

12. Which word correctly completes the sentence?
    Mum and Dad went shopping _____ they are going to have a party for me.
    A so   **B** because
    C if   **D** or

13. Which sentence is punctuated correctly?
    A Where did you put the ball
    B Tell me where you put the ball?
    C Did you find the ball on the grass?
    D The ball is on the grass

14. Which sentence is punctuated correctly?
    A I had a roll an orange, and an apple for lunch.
    B I had a roll, an orange and an apple for lunch?
    C I had a roll, an orange and an apple for lunch!
    D I had a roll, an orange and an apple for lunch.

Answers and explanations on page 121

ANSWERS

Unit 1A — PAGE 8

1. **A**. See line 2.
2. **C**. See line 3.
3. **B**. See line 5.
4. **B**. You can work out that Tom has looked everywhere inside for his cat so now he thinks he'll see if it's outside.
5. **A**. You can work out that the dog is excited to see the cat up in the tree.
6. You can work out that the dog's barking makes Tom think his cat must be up in the tree.

Unit 1B — PAGE 9

1. rug
2. fire
3. look
4. tree
5. Suggested answers: cot, dot, got, hot, lot, not, pot
6. **C**.
7. Where
8. lost
9. **C**.
10. *tree, dog, yard*
11. see
12. in our yard.
13. he
14. I think my cat is lost.
15. You can see the dog from next door.

Unit 1C — PAGE 10

1. **B**.
2. **C**.
3. 1 **B**. 2 **A**. 3 **C**. After Tom loses his cat, he sees a dog barking at a tree and guesses his cat is hiding there.
4. **C**. Tom doesn't give up until he finds his cat. The repeated words show he tries very hard by looking everywhere.
5. **B**. Tom is surprised that the dog has shown him where his cat is while he's looking for it.
6. **A**. Tom takes care to know where his cat is and when she is lost, he goes to a lot of trouble to find her.
7. Responses will vary. Students could draw a picture of Tom looking under the table, under his bed, etc. The caption could be 'Tom looks for his cat' or something similar.

Unit 2A — PAGE 11

1. **B**. See line 2.
2. **C**. See line 3.
3. **B**. See line 5.
4. **A**. You can work out that Libby is happy because she likes to feel more grown up than her brother and she likes her teacher.
5. **C**. You can work out that he is fond of Libby as he calls out to her and looks as if he'd like to climb the fence to be with her.
6. Responses will vary. You could argue that the children need to stay in their own school because if they climbed the fence, no-one would know where anyone was. You may also feel that climbing the fence could be dangerous.

Unit 2B — PAGE 12

1. my
2. come
3. climb
4. little
5. Suggested answers: ban, can, fan, man, nan, pan, ran, tan, van
6. **B**.
7. called
8. sometimes
9. **C**.
10. *head, fingers, fence*
11. started
12. in the playground
13. they
14. I like my new teacher.
15. James likes preschool.

Unit 2C — PAGE 13

1. **B**.
2. **A**.
3. **B**. It is Libby who looks over the fence so they are her eyes.
4. **A**. Libby really means what she says!
5. **C**. They would be pleased to learn that James plays with his friends and Libby likes her new teacher.
6. **B**. Libby guesses that James might climb into her school if he was big enough to get over the fence. She is fond of him but she certainly doesn't want him at her school.

Excel Advanced Skills: Year 1 Advanced English—Answers

7. Responses will vary. It should include a playground with children playing. One child could be waving and calling out "Hello".

Unit 3A — PAGE 14

1. **C**. See line 2.
2. **B**. See line 5.
3. **A**. See line 4.
4. **C**. You can work out that Violet likes Flo because they like doing things together, such as skipping, hopping and looking at the clouds.
5. **A**. You can work out that the things they like doing all take place outside.
6. Responses will vary. Flo is kind to Violet and they enjoy being together. A friend like Flo is a friend you would want to keep forever.

Unit 3B — PAGE 15

1. best
2. eyes
3. bike
4. dragon
5. Suggested answers: bit, fit, hit, kit, lit, pit, sit.
6. C.
7. clouds
8. once
9. D.
10. (labelled picture: clouds, fence, bike)
11. play
12. in the sky
13. they

14. Flo is my best friend.
15. Violet is not as tall as Flo.

Unit 3C — PAGE 16

1. **C**.
2. **B**.
3. **A**. Violet's description of what Flo looks like is in lines 1–2, near the beginning of the text.
4. **A**. The text is all about Violet's thoughts and feelings about her friend.
5. **A**. Flo is a kind person—it is part of her nature.
6. **C**. The picture shows what is in the text: the two friends sitting on the fence looking at the clouds, one a tiny bit taller than the other, with Flo's bike that she rode to Violet's house parked nearby.
7. Responses will vary. The sentence will explain what makes the friend likeable: they could be fun to be with, kind, warm-hearted, etc.

Unit 4A — PAGE 17

1. **C**. See line 2.
2. **B**. See lines 5–6.
3. **B**. See lines 8–9.
4. **A**. You can work out that emus are large birds and small wings would make it difficult for them to lift their bodies in flight.
5. **C**. You can work out that their long legs make it easier for emus to move quickly.
6. **B**. You can work out that eggs need to be kept warm so they incubate. A parent needs to watch over them until they hatch.

Unit 4B — PAGE 18

1. like
2. small
3. emus
4. days
5. Suggested answers: bay, day, hay, lay, may, pay, ray, say
6. A.
7. baby
8. insects
9. C.
10. (labelled picture: neck, feathers, leg)
11. have
12. in the grass
13. he
14. Baby emus hatch from eggs.
15. The emu is a very tall bird.

Unit 4C — PAGE 19

1. **B**.
2. **C**.
3. **C**. The numbers refer to how many eggs are laid (amounts) and how long they take to hatch (length of time).
4. **A**. The describing words (big, tall, brown) are mainly used to tell what emus look like.
5. **A**. The details of how many eggs are laid changes from time to time. The word 'about' helps make this clear.
6. **B**. There is no information in the text about where emus live—their habitat. The picture shows an area where they find food and shelter.

Excel Advanced Skills: Year 1 Advanced English—Answers

ANSWERS

7. Responses will vary. Students may find out, for example, that emus lay large greeny-blue eggs or that their feet have three toes. Students' drawings should illustrate their information.

Unit 5A — PAGE 20

1. **A**. See lines 5–7.
2. **B**. See lines 10–11.
3. **C**. See lines 2–4.
4. **B**. You can work out that she speaks to the children in a friendly, concerned way because she cares about their safety.
5. **B**. You can work out that it is the policewoman's job to make sure the children know the road rules.
6. Responses will vary. If children learn and understand the rules of the road and always follow them carefully, they should stay safe.

Unit 5B — PAGE 21

1. must
2. cross
3. class
4. green
5. Suggested answers: bed, fed, led, red, wed
6. **A**.
7. safety
8. class
9. **C**.
10. *helmet*, *bike*, *road*

11. came
12. on the roads
13. she
14. It is important to know the rules.
15. Does she have a new bike helmet?

Unit 5C — PAGE 22

1. **C**.
2. **A**.
3. 1 **C**. 2 **B**. 3 **A**. George answered first, then Tim and finally the whole class.
4. **A**. The capital letters make the word stand out to show it is important.
5. **B**. You can work out that the students are pleased to show the policewoman they all know this answer.
6. The policewoman calls the children by their names which suggests she has talked to them before.
7. Responses will vary. Other important rules include looking left, right and left again before you cross the road; never running on the road; not crossing the road on a bend; and always wearing your seatbelt.

Unit 6A — PAGE 23

1. **B**. See lines 2–3.
2. **C**. See lines 6–7.
3. **B**. See line 2.
4. **C**. You can work out that three hands with five fingers on each makes fifteen fingers.
5. **A**. You can work out that a child's hand is smaller than an adult's. Also a child is not as tall as an adult and can't reach as high.

6. Responses will vary. Hunting animals for food was a very important part of the lives of Aboriginal people.

Unit 6B — PAGE 24

1. rock
2. hands
3. fingers
4. Australia
5. Suggested answers: bin, din, fin, pin, sin, tin, win
6. **A**.
7. pressed
8. mixture
9. **B**.
10. *finger*, *hand*, *rock*

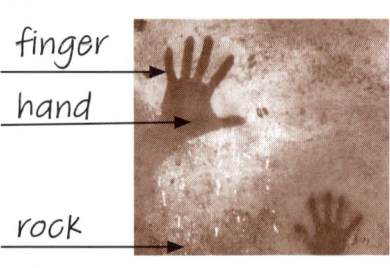

11. was
12. all over the world
13. it
14. Did you see the rock art?
15. They painted pictures of animals.

Unit 6C — PAGE 25

1. **B**.
2. **A**.
3. **B**. The opening sentence gives a definition of rock art.
4. **C**. The third paragraph is the place for this because it is about how prints can be made.
5. **B**. Aboriginal rock art is one kind of rock art. It is different from other rock art.
6. Responses will vary. You might think rock art is interesting because it tells you about what was important in the lives of people thousands of years ago

when they made the art. Or you might think it is only interesting when someone explains what it means.

7. Responses will vary.

Unit 7A — PAGE 26

1. **B**. See line 4.
2. **C**. See line 13.
3. **A**. See line 7.
4. **B**. Stoves can catch fire very easily so it is important to have an adult nearby when children are cooking.
5. **A**. You can work out that you have to pour the mixture into the frying pan so it should be a bit runny.
6. Responses will vary. You might feel there are too many things to measure and you may be afraid to use the stove. Or you might think it is clear what you need to do so this would be easy.

Unit 7B — PAGE 27

1. stove
2. bananas
3. repeat
4. honey
5. Suggested answers: bug, dug, hug, jug, mug, rug, tug
6. **B**.
7. serve
8. adult
9. **D**.
10.
11. need
12. into the pan
13. they
14. We had banana pancakes for breakfast.
15. He did not want nuts or honey.

Unit 7C — PAGE 28

1. **C**.
2. **B**.
3. **B**. You can work out that the list follows the sequence or order in which you will use the ingredients to make the pancakes.
4. **A**. You can work out that it is dangerous to use a stove without an adult nearby so this is an important rule.
5. **C**. Although the utensils are named in the part that tells you what to do, they are not listed anywhere.
6. Responses will vary. You could argue that the picture includes most of the things referred to in the text so it is a good match. Or you could say a picture of cooked pancakes would have been more helpful and inviting.
7. Responses will vary. Suggested answers: toasted cheese sandwiches, Anzac biscuits, glazed honey carrots or guacamole.

NAPLAN-style Reading Test 1 — PAGE 29

1. **C**. See line 2.
2. **A**. See line 2.
3. **B**. See lines 7–8.
4. **B**. Sylvia says she and Ben wore hats. You can also see in the picture that Mum is wearing an apron but not a hat.
5. **A**. The text is about what Sylvia thinks she will be when she grows up.
6. **C**. Sylvia is sure she will be better than Ben at cooking. We don't know what Mum thinks (**B**) and Ben says he does want to be a cook (**A**).
7. **C**. Sylvia's thoughts would be written in a diary. They are not suitable for a magazine or cookbook.

NAPLAN-style Conventions of Language Test 1 — PAGE 30

1. your
2. house
3. friend
4. says
5. should
6. **D**.
7. **A**.
8. **B**.
9. **D**.
10. **C**.
11. into the cup
12. **B**.
13. **A**.
14. **D**.

Unit 8A — PAGE 31

1. **C**. See lines 7–8.
2. **B**. See line 7.
3. **A**. See line 2.
4. **B**. You can work out that Jimmy's parents have said he must put the train set out for sale. Jimmy is worried someone will buy it as he wants to keep it.
5. **C**. You can work out that some objects (e.g. kitchen scales) could interest adults, whereas others (e.g. rollerskates) could interest children; and some (e.g. a cuckoo clock) could interest both.

6. Responses will vary. You might think you'd like to see Jimmy's train set or try his gran's brownies. Or you might dislike garage sales and think there is nothing you'd want to buy.

Unit 8B — PAGE 32

1. kitchen
2. gear
3. chocolate
4. sale
5. Suggested answers: bun, fun, gun, nun, pun, run, sun
6. C.
7. few
8. garage
9. D.
10. years
11. take
12. Saturday 18 June
13. because
14. Will you buy any toys?
15. Have you ever had a garage sale?

Unit 8C — PAGE 33

1. A.
2. B.
3. A. Most of the information is organised under the headings **When**, **Where**, **What** and **Why**.
4. B. The word is emphasised to suggest that almost anything you can think of will be on sale. It is quite common to find this expression in advertisements.
5. C. There is some personal information in the **What** section but the information in the **Why** section is all personal.
6. Responses will vary. Jimmy's parents may think the last sentence (line 10) could turn people off coming to the sale. It is information that isn't suitable in a 'For Sale' notice.
7. Responses will vary. The advertisement will need to include details of when, where and what is for sale, and should avoid personal comments.

Unit 9A — PAGE 34

1. C. See lines 3–4.
2. A. See line 9.
3. B. See line 2.
4. A. You can work out that plastic lasts for hundreds of years so landfill becomes overcrowded.
5. B. If sea creatures eat plastic straws they can die. This is a good reason for humans to ban their use.
6. Responses will vary. It gave her a shock as she realised the problem was even worse than she had thought.

Unit 9B — PAGE 35

1. sister
2. plastic
3. creatures
4. shocked
5. Suggested answers: die, lie, pie, tie
6. B.
7. ban
8. once
9. D.
10. straws
11. think
12. last week
13. because
14. Can you snorkel?
15. Will you stop using plastic straws?

Unit 9C — PAGE 36

1. A.
2. A.
3. B. The information about the sister is personal and not suitable for an encyclopedia.
4. C. It is clear that the writer feels very strongly about banning plastic straws because it leads to the death of sea creatures.
5. B. A circle with a line through it means it is banned. This picture means that no plastic straws are allowed here.
6. Responses will vary. A likely answer is yes, because it is easy to drink without a straw and plastic straws can cause the death of animals.
7. Responses will vary. A circle with a picture of a dog and a line through it will be effective.

Unit 10A — PAGE 37

1. C. See line 3.
2. B. See line 4.
3. A. See line 9.
4. A. You can work out that the milk needs to be pumped out of the udders so it can be collected.
5. C. You can work out that the word 'roughly' shows it is a similar amount but not exactly the same.
6. A. You can work out that, since the text says most milk comes from cows, it can't be true that all milk comes from cows. Milk also comes from other animals.

Unit 10B — PAGE 38

1. cream
2. machines
3. calf
4. udders
5. Suggested answers: bow, cow, how, now, row, wow
6. A.
7. cud
8. roughly
9. B.
10. machines
11. comes
12. every day
13. and
14. Did you see our newborn calves?
15. We make cheese, cream and butter at our farm.

Unit 10C — PAGE 39

1. C.
2. A.
3. B. You can work out that each sentence in the paragraph is about cows and their milk.
4. C. You can work out that there is other important information about cows that is not in this text.
5. B. You can work out that there isn't a description of what cows look like in the words of the text. You can only see what they look like in the picture.
6. A. Each sentence gives the reader factual information about cows.
7. Responses will vary. If you shake for the full length of time you will make butter. There will also be some liquid called buttermilk.

Unit 11A — PAGE 40

1. C. See line 2.
2. B. See lines 2–3.
3. B. See lines 11–12.
4. A. You can work out that Melanie must have read it before since it is one of her 'favourite books'.
5. C. You can work out that the dog changes from sad to lucky once Jack is his owner.
6. B. You can work out that one reason she likes it so much is because of the feelings she has when reading it.

Unit 11B — PAGE 41

1. today
2. laugh
3. owner
4. knitted
5. Suggested answers: bad, dad, fad, had, lad, mad, pad, sad
6. B.
7. my
8. laugh
9. C.
10. books
11. knitted
12. by the end
13. but
14. What is your favourite book?
15. Has Tom read this book yet?

Unit 11C — PAGE 42

1. B.
2. B.
3. A. The middle section lists several reasons why the book is Melanie's favourite.
4. C. When sad refers to a feeling it doesn't have a capital letter but when Sad is a name (a proper noun) it needs a capital letter.
5. B. Melanie writes about her favourite book so this would make a good title for her text.
6. Responses will vary. Students might say they wouldn't like it because they don't like to be made to feel sad. Or they might say they would like it because they love stories about dogs with good pictures.
7. Responses will vary. Suggested answer: *The Three Billy Goats Gruff*—I like this story because it is scary but has a happy ending.

Unit 12A — PAGE 43

1. A. See line 2.
2. C. See line 11.
3. B. See lines 2–4.
4. A. You can work out that it is taking pollen from one plant to another that causes new plants to grow.
5. B. You can work out that if sprays which are harmful to bees were used, the bees could die.
6. Responses will vary. Without bees many flowers, vegetables and fruits would not grow because they would not receive the pollen they need.

Unit 12B — PAGE 44

1. garden
2. water
3. sprays
4. pollen
5. Suggested answers: boo, loo, moo, poo, roo, too, zoo

6. **D.**
7. shallow
8. provide
9. **C.**
10. gardens
11. carry
12. at any time
13. so
14. Do you have bees in your garden?
15. We grow flowers, fruit and vegetables.

Unit 12C PAGE 45

1. **C.**
2. **A.**
3. **B.** Paragraph two explains some of the ways in which we can be helpful to bees.
4. **C.** 1 Don't use harmful sprays. 2 Grow plants that bees like. 3 Provide water for the bees. 4 Add a rock for the bees' safe landing.
5. Responses will vary. They are visiting lavender plants to get nectar and pollen from them.
6. You can work out that some other insects, such as butterflies, carry pollen and the wind could blow it so it lands on other plants.
7. Yes; After a bee stings, it dies.

Unit 13A PAGE 46

1. **B.** See line 9.
2. **A.** See lines 4–5.
3. **C.** See lines 9–10.
4. **C.** You can work out that The Glower is a new product which hasn't been on sale before.
5. **B.** The writer claims Bill's teeth glow with health and shine but they just look odd!
6. Responses will vary. You might not want to buy The Glower as you think the whole advertisement is a joke. Or you might like to try it to see what the fuss is about.

Unit 13B PAGE 47

1. health
2. toothpaste
3. Everyone
4. right
5. Suggested answers: cop, hop, lop, mop, top
6. **D.**
7. shine
8. glowing
9. **D.**
10. teeth
11. is
12. right now
13. because
14. Have you bought yours yet?
15. Don't you like Bill's smile?

Unit 13C PAGE 48

1. **A.**
2. **B.**
3. **A.** You can work out that the speaker wants each viewer to become a buyer. A way to do this is to make the viewer feel special. Putting 'YOU' in capital letters achieves this.
4. **A.** You can work out that the speaker wants the viewers to wish they were just like the people with healthy, shiny teeth who have their lives changed for the better.
5. **A.** You can work out that the claims made for the toothpaste are exaggerated and would never happen.
6. Responses will vary. The picture is an amusing cartoon-like image. It suggests the text might be more of a joke about how silly some advertisements are than a serious advertisement.
7. Responses will vary. Advertisements that appeal could include ones for food, drinks, toys, games and things you want to collect. If they are for products that are new on the market, popular with others, on sale or a new trend they could also catch your interest.

Unit 14A PAGE 49

1. **B.** See lines 2–3.
2. **C.** See line 13.
3. **B.** See line 11.
4. **C.** You can work out that they can vary their food but they will always need water.
5. **A.** You can work out that it is important to remember where you hid your food if food is scarce.
6. Responses will vary. Making tools and using them is something humans do. It is very clever for a bird to be able to do this.

Unit 14B PAGE 50

1. feathers
2. each
3. memories
4. information
5. Suggested answers: bet, get, let, met, net, pet, set, vet, wet
6. **C.**
7. nearby
8. tools
9. **A.**
10. feathers

11. have
12. months earlier
13. and
14. She saw the crow pick up the worm.
15. Are there crows where you live?

Unit 14C — PAGE 51

1. **C**.
2. **B**.
3. **C**. The third paragraph is about clever things crows can do.
4. **B**. There is no information about the ways crows look after their babies.
5. **A**. The word chat is generally used to describe people having a friendly talk with each other.
6. **B**. There is nothing shy about the way crows behave: they are noisy and nothing stops them getting what they want.
7. Responses will vary. Suggested answers: "What's for dinner?"; "We just need some rubber to finish off our nest."

Unit 15A — PAGE 52

1. **C**. See line 5.
2. **B**. See lines 6–7.
3. **A**. See lines 2–3.
4. **B**. You can work out that Bobby is still wondering what to call his kitten when he asks "What shall I call you, little kitten?".
5. **A**. You can work out that cats don't understand the wording of questions but they can show they understand friendly, gentle behaviour by meowing.
6. Responses will vary. It is likely Bobby will do most things as he is so keen to look after the kitten well. But it is easy to forget some things like keeping the food dishes washed.

Unit 15B — PAGE 53

1. sixth
2. present
3. kitten
4. fur
5. Suggested answers: bum, gum, hum, mum, rum, sum
6. **C**.
7. perhaps
8. best
9. **D**.
10. tray
11. teach
12. every day
13. so
14. Have you seen my kitten?
15. I think Bobby will love his kitten.

Unit 15C — PAGE 54

1. **A**.
2. **C**.
3. **A**. Bobby asks his parents for a kitten before he gets one for his birthday.
4. **B**. The exclamation mark stresses how much Bobby wants a kitten.
5. **A**. Bobby knows how little and new his kitten is so he speaks gently to it.
6. Responses will vary. It suits the text because the kitten looks just like the one Bobby describes and it looks ready to play games with Bobby.
7. Responses will vary. The name is the student's choice but to suit the kitten it needs to be a warm, friendly or playful name such as Fuzzy or Buddy or even Meow!

NAPLAN-style Reading Test 2 — PAGE 55

1. **C**. See line 4.
2. **C**. See lines 8–9.
3. **B**. See lines 10–11.
4. **A**. They dive from tree branches to the ground to catch insects and small animals in their bills.
5. **C**. The text is full of factual information.
6. **B**. Their regular calls are like clockwork telling the listeners it is sunrise or sunset.
7. **B**. The brackets show the sentence gives information that is helpful but not directly about kookaburras.

NAPLAN-style Conventions of Language Test 2 — PAGE 56

1. their
2. Everybody
3. honey
4. parents
5. school
6. **C**.
7. **B**.
8. **D**.
9. **C**.
10. **A**.
11. **D**.
12. **C**.
13. **D**.
14. **A**.

Unit 16A — PAGE 57

1. **B**. See lines 5–7.
2. **A**. See lines 2–4.
3. **C**. See lines 14–16.
4. **A**. The fact that she drinks her mother's milk shows she must be a baby as that is how mothers and babies behave.

Excel Advanced Skills: Year 1 Advanced English—Answers

5. **B.** You can work out that some giraffes have babies in the wild and in zoos without going on road trips.
6. **C.** The writer shows concern that giraffes could die out but when a new baby giraffe is born, the writer feels more hopeful that this won't happen.

Unit 16B — PAGE 58

1. giraffe
2. road
3. wobbly
4. choose
5. Suggested answers: bill, dill, fill, gill, hill, mill, pill, sill, till
6. **C.**
7. competition
8. across
9. **A.**
10. Kitoto
11. is
12. safely
13. she
14. Well done, Kitoto!
15. That's wonderful news!

Unit 16C — PAGE 59

1. **B.**
2. **B.**
3. **A.** The first paragraph explains why the trip was necessary.
4. **B.** The picture shows a baby giraffe drinking from her mother. The second paragraph refers to this idea.
5. **C.** The central good news story is that a new-born giraffe has been born in a zoo—something that doesn't happen often.
6. Responses will vary. You can work out that the zoo wants people to know that we need more baby giraffes as they could die out. A competition to name the baby will be popular and make people take notice.
7. Responses will vary. Suggested answers: Their mothers stand to give birth so that the babies fall on their heads when they are born (it makes them take their first breath); their little horns are born flat but soon stand up straight; they can stand and then run within hours of being born.

Unit 17A — PAGE 60

1. **C.** See line 2.
2. **B.** See line 8.
3. **C.** See line 3.
4. **C.** You can work out that Yoda is going to the place where he will be a guide dog about a year after he began his training.
5. **B.** You can work out that Yoda is looking forward to being a help to someone and using his new skills.
6. Responses will vary. It is likely Yoda will be an excellent guide dog as he has been well trained and is keen to be helpful.

Unit 17B — PAGE 61

1. guide
2. nearly
3. someone
4. able
5. Suggested answers: book, cook, hook, nook, rook, sook, took
6. **D.**
7. guide
8. right
9. **A.**
10. Monroes
11. am
12. badly
13. they
14. I'm so excited!
15. They take me for a walk every day.

Unit 17C — PAGE 62

1. **C.**
2. **A.**
3. **C.** Yoda is referring to her first job as a guide dog when she says she can't wait. The sentence needs to follow the information about this in paragraph two.
4. **B.** Although both families are mentioned, the text gives Yoda's account of learning to be a guide dog.
5. **A.** Yoda has high praise for the care given by all the Monroes.
6. Responses will vary. You can see Yoda has to wear a harness when he is at training and you can see he is comfortable around other dogs.
7. Responses will vary. The writing should be in the first person (I, we) to give the thoughts and feelings of the animal chosen.

Unit 18A — PAGE 63

1. **C.** See line 3.
2. **A.** See lines 4–5.
3. **A.** See lines 6–7.
4. **C.** You can work out that, since the aim of the game is to get the highest score, it would be better to kick a goal than a point.
5. **B.** You can work out that there are two goalposts and one post on each side of them, making four in total.
6. Responses will vary. Suggested answers: kicking goals or helping others in your team to kick goals; stopping people in the team you are playing against from kicking goals.

Unit 18B — PAGE 64

1. teams
2. goal
3. special
4. women's
5. Suggested answers: came, dame, fame, lame, name, same, tame
6. A.
7. special
8. players
9. C.
10. Australia
11. wore
12. skilfully
13. she
14. Our team kicked ten goals today!
15. I asked my friend to play Aussie Rules with me.

Unit 18C — PAGE 65

1. A.
2. B.
3. C. This is new information that doesn't fit with the contents of paragraphs one or two.
4. B. The word is an adjective that describes the kind of rules the game follows.
5. A. To be a star in this game you need to stand out from others by playing very well.
6. Responses will vary. You might love playing with a team because you like working together with others or you might not like it because you worry you'll let down your team.
7. Responses will vary. Words and images could be related to where you were born, where you live, family members, pets, things you play with or collect, and so on.

Unit 19A — PAGE 66

1. C. See lines 2–3.
2. C. See lines 8–9.
3. B. See lines 9–10.
4. A. You can work out that the rules would vary as each game has its own rules (lines 11–12).
5. C. You can work out that what is unusual about these games is they are eaten as you play.
6. Responses will vary. You might think it would be disappointing not to have your game left when you finish playing. Or you might like the idea of bringing together two things you enjoy doing—eating and playing games.

Unit 19B — PAGE 67

1. might
2. Australian
3. supermarket
4. board
5. Suggested answers: bind, find, hind, mind, rind, wind
6. A.
7. idea
8. board
9. C.
10. Chocolateland
11. are
12. easily
13. they
14. You can even eat the board!
15. What did the dice taste like?

Unit 19C — PAGE 68

1. C.
2. B.
3. A. The writer is asking a question of 'you', the person reading the text.
4. B. To eat the board you play on is a new, surprising idea.
5. B. The new games you can eat have the word 'land' in their titles. Snakes and Ladders doesn't and it is also an old game.
6. Responses will vary. The picture shows that all the family can take part in these games—they are not just for children.
7. Responses will vary. Suggested answers: Marshmallowland, Vegemiteontoastland or Bananaland.

Unit 20A — PAGE 69

1. C. See line 2.
2. B. See lines 3–5.
3. B. See line 6.
4. A. You can work out that the diets of bats vary, which means there are different types of bats.
5. C. Humans can't fly using their own power whereas bats can.
6. Responses will vary. Bats can look rather spooky and unattractive (as the poet implies); they also behave in odd ways and could look scary flying together in the night sky.

Unit 20B — PAGE 70

1. umbrella
2. mammals
3. blossoms
4. mainly
5. Suggested answers: bang, fang, gang, pang, rang, sang, tang
6. B.
7. prefer
8. only
9. D.
10. Australia
11. have
12. together
13. you

Excel Advanced Skills: Year 1 Advanced English—Answers

115

14. Bats sleep upside down!
15. Some bats eat insects, frogs and mice.

Unit 20C — PAGE 71

1. **A**.
2. **A**.
3. **C**. It is a way of helping the reader think about the information.
4. **B**. The poet describes what the bats look like by comparing them with things he thinks they are similar to (umbrella spokes; old rags).
5. **C**. The poet's words suggest he finds bats rather ugly and something to avoid.
6. Responses will vary. The writer doesn't share the poet's distaste for bats and has some admiration for their usefulness to humans.
7. Responses will vary. Suggested answers:
   When spiders are asleep they look like commas or full stops.
   When baby snakes are asleep they look like old, thin shoelaces.
   When wombats are asleep they look like plump, brown cushions.

Unit 21A — PAGE 72

1. **A**. See lines 3 and 6.
2. **B**. See lines 8 and 11.
3. **B**. See lines 7 and 20.
4. **B**. You can work out that you can use any food colouring of your choice as no particular colour is suggested.
5. **A**. It can be dangerous for a child to use a stove so it is wise to have a parent nearby in case anything goes wrong.
6. Responses will vary. Suggested answers: figures of animals or people, bowls and dishes, jewellery.

Unit 21B — PAGE 73

1. bowl
2. wooden
3. knead
4. ingredients
5. Suggested answers: beat, feat, meat, neat, seat, teat
6. **C**.
7. clump
8. medium
9. **D**.
10. Jupiter
11. leave
12. often
13. it
14. She asked what I made with the clay.
15. You will need a pot, a bowl and a spoon.

Unit 21C — PAGE 74

1. **B**.
2. **A**.
3. **B**. It is useful to have everything ready before you begin to make the clay.
4. **B**. If the steps were done in a different order you wouldn't get the same results at the end. No clay!
5. **C**. They are verbs that tell you what to do.
6. Responses will vary. The picture shows children playing with clay that has already been made. Their clay has been made with different food colourings.
7. Responses will vary. Suggested answers:
   Ingredients: two or three oranges
   Utensils: orange squeezer, glass
   What to do: Cut oranges in half, squeeze juice from oranges, pour juice into glass

Unit 22A — PAGE 75

1. **C**. See lines 2–3.
2. **B**. See lines 6–8.
3. **B**. See lines 7–8.
4. **A**. You can work out that when you say the sentence quickly, it is the 's' and 'sh' sounds that run together when you say them.
5. Responses will vary. Suggested answer: to make funny mixed-up sounds can make you laugh at your mistakes, especially when you are trying not to get muddled.
6. Responses will vary. Mary is unlikely to think a tongue twister about her would last for such a long time. She would certainly be surprised.

Unit 22B — PAGE 76

1. sentence
2. knot
3. tongue
4. young
5. Suggested answers: dear, fear, gear, hear, rear, tear, year
6. **C**.
7. fossils
8. sounds
9. **C**.
10. Fred
11. saying
12. quickly
13. he
14. He said, "Fred fed Ted bread."
15. That's a shock!

Unit 22C — PAGE 77

1. B.
2. A.
3. A. The best place for the definition is at the very beginning.
4. A. There are 't' sounds at the beginning of each word and in the middle of the second word.
5. C. This links the man's confused state with his efforts at trying to untwist his tongue twisters!
6. B. The 'sh' and 'ch' sounds are the ones that are difficult to say quickly when close together.
7. Responses will vary.

Unit 23A — PAGE 78

1. B. See lines 5–6.
2. C. See line 9.
3. B. See line 11.
4. A. You can work out that the bees are storing this as food for the hive when nectar is in short supply.
5. B. You can work out that bees work very hard to gather, carry and safely store the nectar.
6. Responses will vary. Humans take the honeycombs from the hives and then prepare them to be kept in jars as honey.

Unit 23B — PAGE 79

1. honey
2. stomachs
3. chewed
4. honeycomb
5. Suggested answers: begins, began, begun, beginning
6. C.
7. seal
8. tongues
9. C.
10. the flowers
11. find
12. carefully
13. so
14. What beautiful honey!
15. Where do bees store nectar?

Unit 23C — PAGE 80

1. B.
2. C.
3. A. The writer talks directly to the reader so they will think about what is being said.
4. B. Terms such as 'wax-like tubes' and 'beeswax' are scientific.
5. A. You can work out that the writer is impressed by what the bees do to make honey.
6. Responses will vary. The text describes a real process and needs a picture which explains more about the process. This picture is bright and cheerful but it doesn't suit the text because it is cartoon-like and not realistic.
7. A honey bee has six legs, three body parts (head, thorax and abdomen) and two sets of wings.

NAPLAN-style Reading Test 3 — PAGE 81

1. A. See lines 5–6.
2. C. See lines 10–11.
3. B. See lines 10–11.
4. A. The choice King Midas makes is very foolish as it could have led to disaster for him and his family.
5. B. King Midas doesn't realise that things like the food he wants to eat or the water he wants to drink would turn to gold. The discovery would have been horrifying to him as he could die and his daughter could remain a statue.
6. A. He is greedy rather than evil. He loves his daughter and doesn't mean to harm her. He is kind to a visitor. He learns his lesson and changes into a better person—something someone truly evil would not do.
7. C. King Midas got exactly what he wished for!

NAPLAN-style Conventions of Language Test 3 — PAGE 82

1. father
2. children
3. threw
4. Where
5. sugar
6. A.
7. B.
8. C.
9. Sally
10. C.
11. greedily
12. C.
13. C.
14. B.

Unit 24A — PAGE 83

1. C. See lines 1–2.
2. B. See lines 10–11.
3. A. See lines 7–8.
4. A. You can work out that some people think Josephine is wasting her time dreaming about being a dancer. Kangaroos are not born to be dancers.
5. C. You can work out that Maximo thinks people would prefer to find out about the surprise for themselves.
6. Responses will vary. Josephine doesn't give up. She holds on to her dream and doesn't listen to people who tell her she's silly.

Unit 24B   PAGE 84

1. dancer
2. dream
3. favourite
4. laugh
5. Suggested answers: dances, danced, dancing, dancer, dancers, danceable
6. A.
7. musical
8. end
9. B.
10. a kangaroo
11. see
12. in the bush
13. and
14. Do you have a favourite book?
15. I've never seen a dancing kangaroo!

Unit 24C   PAGE 85

1. B.
2. A.
3. B, A and C.
4. A. It isn't easy to keep doing something when others laugh at you. Maximo thinks Josephine's determination is admirable.
5. Responses will vary. Josephine's dream is to be a dancer even though no-one believes kangaroos can be dancers.
6. Responses will vary. Maximo says Josephine's surprise is 'wonderful'. This comes near the end of the book so it sounds as if there is a happy ending.
7. Responses will vary. Suggested answer:
   I Want My Hat Back by Jon Klassen
   You think it is going to be like other stories but it turns out to be very different. It also has a very funny surprise at the end.

Unit 25A   PAGE 86

1. C. See line 2.
2. B. See line 4.
3. C. See lines 4–6.
4. B. You can work out that even a tall adult couldn't wrap their arms around a two-and-a half-metre tree trunk.
5. C. You can work out that if two and a half metres is two huge steps plus a small one, then one metre is roughly one huge step. Roots can grow to 9 metres or 9 huge steps.
6. Responses will vary. Suggested answers: Animals who feed on their fruits find them useful. They also provide shelter and shade.

Unit 25B   PAGE 87

1. size
2. half
3. Possums
4. fruit
5. Suggested answers: grows, grew, growing, grower, growth
6. B.
7. famous
8. spread
9. C.
10. the soil
11. climbed
12. At times
13. because
14. Do possums eat the figs?
15. There's a Moreton Bay Fig tree in our park.

Unit 25C   PAGE 88

1. A.
2. C.
3. B. The measurements of the parts of the tree are given in this paragraph.
4. A. You can work out that the writer chooses things the reader will know the size of (big steps, a giraffe) to make it easier for the reader to tell how big parts of the tree are.
5. C. Giraffes are tall so it is amazing to learn that a tree can grow many times taller than a giraffe.
6. B. The tree makes the human figures look very small so you realise how large the tree is.
7. Responses will vary. Aboriginal people are said to have eaten the figs; used bark to make bags or to weave fishing nets; and used the branches to make dugout canoes.

Unit 26A   PAGE 89

1. A. See line 2.
2. C. See line 6.
3. C. See lines 18–19.
4. B. You can work out that the duck feels it is stuck in its boring old pond and wishes it could see more of the world.
5. B. You can work out that the Duck envies the Kangaroo's freedom to roam the world, hopping through fields and water.
6. Responses will vary. Suggested answer: The kangaroo takes the Duck on journeys around the world so it is no longer bored.

Unit 26B   PAGE 90

1. hopped
2. moonlight
3. quite
4. tail
5. Suggested answers: sell, sells, selling, sales, sold
6. B.
7. whole

8. balance
9. A.
10. the Kangaroo
11. said
12. at the end of my tail
13. or
14. 'Will you take me with you?' I asked.
15. 'I wish I could hop like you,' he said.

Unit 26C — PAGE 91

1. A.
2. B.
3. 1 B. 2 A. 3 C. The Duck sees what fun the Kangaroo has and accepts its offer to get on its tail so they can travel the world together.
4. A. You can work out that **pale** would usually come before the word **moonlight** but in the poem it comes after it to make the rhyme with **tail**.
5. C. The poem is a fantasy about a Duck and a Kangaroo. It takes place in the poet's imagination and is not at all serious.
6. Responses will vary. Suggested answers: The Duck likes to complain and ask for what it wants; the Kangaroo is a bit fussy but is willing to please the Duck.
7. Responses will vary. You might give it five stars because it makes you laugh and you like the way it bounces along with its cheery rhythm. Or you might give it only one star because you think it is just a lot of nonsense!

Unit 27A — PAGE 92

1. C. See lines 1–3.
2. A. See line 10.
3. C. See lines 7–8.
4. A. You can work out that the only block of colour in the picture of Peter is his jacket.
5. B. You can work out that Tim thought Peter Rabbit had come to life from a storybook he knew.
6. Responses will vary. You might think Tim saw a rabbit he thought was Peter. Or you might think Tim imagined he saw him.

Unit 27B — PAGE 93

1. tail
2. carrots
3. believed
4. replied
5. Suggested answers: plays, played, playing, player, players
6. A.
7. believed
8. forgot
9. C.
10. the rabbit/Peter Rabbit
11. come
12. in his garden
13. or
14. I've read a story about Peter Rabbit.
15. "Have as many as you want," said Tim.

Unit 27C — PAGE 94

1. B.
2. C.
3. B. The actual time when the story took place is not given. Once upon a time means a time in the past.
4. A. The tail and a powder puff are similar because they are both soft and fluffy to the touch.
5. A. Tim thinks the rabbit is Peter from his storybook but he hasn't really met him before. He decides to speak to him as if he knows him which is quite brave.
6. Responses will vary. You might like stories about storybook characters coming to life. Or you might think the story needed to be longer and have more action in it.
7. Responses will vary. For example, you might like to talk to Max from *Where the Wild Things Are* and ask him to tell you more about the wild things.

Unit 28A — PAGE 95

1. B. See lines 3–4.
2. C. See lines 15–16.
3. A. See line 5.
4. A. You can see in the picture that there are antlers on the dragon's head.
5. A. You can work out that the dragons in the streets at Chinese New Year are really people in dragon costumes.
6. Responses will vary. Chinese people admire dragons and believe they can bring good luck.

Unit 28B — PAGE 96

1. dragon
2. Chinese
3. scales
4. Its
5. Suggested answers: races, raced, racing, racer, racers
6. C.
7. part

119

Excel Advanced Skills: Year 1 Advanced English—Answers

8. Chinese
9. D.
10. The paddles
11. is
12. in China
13. and
14. Chinese New Year is held early in the year.
15. The dragon parade was very exciting!

Unit 28C — PAGE 97

1. B.
2. A.
3. C. Until the last sentence, paragraph 3 is about what the boat looks like. This means the sentence should be placed in this paragraph but before the more general statement that concludes it.
4. B. These words are special terms to make clear which part of a boat is being talked about. They are important terms for sailors to use.
5. C. The action of paddling is similar to rowing. Both are also team sports.
6. Responses will vary. You might think you couldn't paddle fast enough or would be scared. Or you might think it would be exciting and fun to be in a boatrace with other people.
7. Responses will vary. Suggested answer: People are scared of my dragon because it is fierce and evil.

Unit 29A — PAGE 98

1. B. See line 2.
2. A. See line 9.
3. C. See lines 5–6.
4. C. You can work out that they wanted to rescue Trim from drowning.
5. B. You can work out that Flinders was a daring, clever sea captain who sailed where others had not sailed.
6. Responses will vary. Most cats can't swim and most cats don't travel the world on a boat with someone famous.

Unit 29B — PAGE 99

1. litter
2. white
3. chosen
4. overboard
5. Suggested answers: write, writes, written, writing
6. A.
7. several
8. litter
9. C.
10. a ship
11. fell
12. like greased lightning
13. but
14. Cat overboard!
15. The captain named his cat Trim.

Unit 29C — PAGE 100

1. B.
2. C.
3. 1 C. 2 A. 3 B. The text begins by telling where and when Trim was born. It goes on to describe what he looked like and then to outline what happened in his life.
4. A. The idea suggested is that even though Trim was mainly a black cat, his feet were white all over. It made him look as if someone had dipped his black feet in snow.
5. Responses will vary. Trim is all black in the statue but the text explains he has some white patches.
6. Responses will vary. Flinders chose Trim from the litter and kept the cat with him over several long voyages. He describes him with affection and sounds very fond of him.
7. Harriet (He was called Harry at first!); Donna

Unit 30A — PAGE 101

1. C. See line 5.
2. A. See lines 3–4.
3. B. See lines 10–11.
4. A. You can work out that there is an explanation for being unable to see the moon in the day. It hasn't been eaten or disappeared; it is there but it can't be seen at that time.
5. B. You can work out that the question has no answer because it is asking about something that only happens in the writer's imagination!
6. Responses will vary. Both the titles are questions but the questions are of different kinds. The first needs a serious answer: an explanation about something that happens in the real world. The second is a joke because it makes the search for an answer like a whodunnit. In fact there is no answer because what is described hasn't happened. The titles look similar but they work differently.

Unit 30B   PAGE 102

1. shiny
2. someone
3. please
4. scarcely
5. Suggested answers: hear, hears, hearing, hearer
6. A.
7. where
8. nowhere
9. B.
10. the day
11. are
12. in the night
13. but
14. It's quite a puzzle.
15. Everyone knows the moon's made of cheese!

Unit 30C   PAGE 103

1. B.
2. A.
3. B. Although the poems were written 100 years apart, it doesn't matter which order you read them in. They express different thoughts about the moon.
4. C. Neither text offers an answer to the question asked.
5. Responses will vary. The quarter moon in the picture illustrates the idea that someone has taken a large bite out of the moon as in Text 2. The moon shines brightly against the darkness in the picture so this also suits Text 1. Or you could argue the picture is realistic and so suits Text 1 but not Text 2 as that needs a comical, cartoon-like illustration.
6. Responses will vary. You might decide you like the way Text 1 asks an important question in a friendly, simple way where Text 2 is just a joke. Or you might think the humour of Text 2 is witty and amusing, and Text 1 is not as interesting or imaginative.
7. Responses will vary. The rhyme schemes of Text 1 (abcb) and Text 2 (aabb) provide models or you might use an aaaa pattern for your four lines.

NAPLAN-style Reading Test 4   PAGE 104

1. C. See lines 2–4.
2. C. See lines 5–6.
3. B. You can work out that if it had fallen from the bin it would have landed on the ground.
4. A. You can work out that the possum's problem was that it couldn't get its head out of the jar—it was stuck inside it.
5. C. You can see in the picture that a possum's feet have sharp claws. The towel stops its claws scratching the officer.
6. C. You can work out that this is a news report.
7. B. You can work out that if Joel hadn't seen the possum was in trouble and gone for help, it may have died.

NAPLAN-style Conventions of Language Test 4   PAGE 105

1. sail
2. only
3. because
4. Would
5. many
6. C.
7. A.
8. B.
9. D.
10. C.
11. D.
12. B.
13. C.
14. D.

Excel Advanced Skills: Year 1 Advanced English—Answers

NOTES

NOTES

© 2021 Pascal Press

ISBN 978 1 74125 647 5

Pascal Press
PO Box 250
Glebe NSW 2037
(02) 8585 4044
www.pascalpress.com.au

Publisher: Vivienne Joannou
Project editor: Mark Dixon
Edited and proofread by Mark Dixon
Answers checked by Dale Little
Cover and page design by Sonia Woo
Typeset by Grizzly Graphics (Leanne Richters)
Printed by Vivar Printing/Green Giant Press

Reproduction and communication for educational purposes
The Australian *Copyright Act 1968* (the Act) allows a maximum of one chapter or 10% of the pages of this work, whichever is the greater, to be reproduced and/or communicated by any educational institution for its educational purposes provided that the educational institution (or the body that administers it) has given a remuneration notice to Copyright Agency under the Act.

For details of the Copyright Agency licence for educational institutions contact:

Copyright Agency
Level 12, 66 Goulburn Street
Sydney NSW 2000
Telephone: (02) 9394 7600
Facsimile: (02) 9394 7601
Email: memberservices@copyright.com.au

Reproduction and communication for other purposes
Except as permitted under the Act (for example, a fair dealing for the purposes of study, research, criticism or review) no part of this book may be reproduced, stored in a retrieval system, communicated or transmitted in any form or by any means without prior written permission. All inquiries should be made to the publisher at the address above.

All efforts to contact individuals regarding copyright have been made and permission acknowledged where applicable. In the event of any oversight, please contact the publisher so correction can be made in subsequent editions.